D1101555

EXHIBITION PLANNING AND DESIGN

EXHIBITION PLANNING AND DESIGN

A Guide for Exhibitors, Designers and Contractors

John Allwood and Bryan Montgomery

B. T. Batsford Ltd · *London*

Typeset by Tameside Filmsetting, Ltd.
Ashton-under-Lyne, Lancs.
and printed in Great Britain at
The Bath Press, Avon

Published by B. T. Batsford Ltd
4 Fitzhardinge Street,
London WIH OAH

Contents

The colour sections follow pages 32 and 96.

Preface

Once upon a time many years ago John Allwood came to my office to talk about the great exhibitions of the past; and especially Wembley. He struck an instant chord with me because my history tutor E. A. Belcher had visited Australia and New Zealand expressly to persuade those great Dominions to take part in the British Empire Exhibition of 1924 at Wembley.

At our meeting John and I developed the idea of a joint book to combine our common interests in exhibition stand design and exhibition stand management, to be aimed particularly at those people who were suddenly landed with partial responsibility for arranging their company's 'exhibitions'.

Over the next year we developed the synopsis together and the glossary. John was often in Vancouver where he had been appointed by Ted Allen of the Central Office of Information to develop plans for the British Pavilion for the 1986 World Expo. In 1984 John contracted leukaemia and started the first of many visits to hospital. Throughout his treatments and the enforced periods of rest he dictated the raw material for this book on to tape. He continued this task right up until his final illness and death in December 1985. His last instruction to me was to arrange for a photographer to take the series of site photographs which appear in this book, every day from the same position at Interbuild.

The final selection of photographs had therefore to be made without his help. I turned to Mike Howitt, who had developed with us his series of courses on promoting sensible and effective design and management of exhibition stands, for bad and indifferent practice from many different exhibitions in many different exhibition halls. Inevitably the selection of photographs and the points made by them are my personal choice.

To those exhibitors who recognise themselves or their companies, I hope you approve of the captions finally selected.

Much of the text was developed from the two films made by Video Arts. The first one 'How not to exhibit yourself' was made by us jointly and worked out with Tony Jay. We created a film set in the form of a stand at one of our exhibitions, shooting the scenes after hours and with immediate access to real life extras during the exhibition itself. The next film about planning exhibition participation dealt with a typical project and was called 'It'll be OK on the day'. Both these films have been seen worldwide, and also shown in a number of national television programmes. As well as being good fun, they have no doubt added considerably to the greater degree of professionalism at trade exhibitions and to the consequential increase in exhibitors' success stories. With Video Arts we combined the text messages into a booklet designed to accompany the films into the training armoury of marketing and sales management.

So from lectures, theatrical performances and films, finally to this book. John and I both saw the book not as a beginning to end story – it hardly makes a rattling good read. Rather we saw it as a place for dipping, a source of greater encouragement for everyone out to make an impression for their company and a reminder that other people have experienced the same agonies, anxieties and final success.

Acknowledgements

Many cooks had a hand in this broth; either by contributing from their experiences or by encouragement when writer's block struck again. Charles Owen was one of the first with his idea for a Magnum Opus for the exhibitor and long after referred to it as the Mopus. Then came a series of articles for UNIDO in the form of Trade Show Tips produced by John Vimpany, Ian Grimshaw, Denis Casson, Peter Evans and Simon Osborn.

Alan Taylor and Ian Saunders were largely responsible for assembling the part three section. Adrian Camu, Naomi Gorrick and Peter Evans started and finished the assembly of pieces and provided much needed pressure at the right points.

The photographs mostly came from Mike Howitt, although he might be surprised to read the captions that I put under his sometimes astringent and probably libellous situations. Video Arts' wonderful approch comes through to me all the time. Tony Jay, John Cleese and Denis Norden produced sentences and *bon mots* that have come into our exhibition culture and are frequently quoted with recognition and enjoyment – 'The key to the drink cupboard to remain in the possession of the stand manager at all times'. Many other Video Arts films have a relevance to exhibiting as well as marketing and dealing with people.

Finally, John and I would like to thank Jenny Towndrow and the Society of Industrial Artists and Designers for this initial commission and subsequently Michael Sadler-Forster and the Chartered Society of Designers for the agreement with Batsford in the person of Tony Seward, their senior Academic Editor.

If this book is entirely readable it is due to the enthusiasm and light touch of David Dean; a master wordsmith without whom this book would have been turgid, ungrammatical and pedestrian. May you go from prologue to epilogue with success.

Bryan Montgomery   November 1988
Manchester Square
London

Prologue

'Exhibitions? No, not our scene, really. Too difficult, I'm afraid, and too expensive. Months of chaos, and no way of evaluating the result in the end.'

Our aim in this book is to lead such conventional spirits out of their timid preconceptions and into a real and exciting world. Of course, success does not ordinarily come about by accident, in exhibiting any more than in most other fields: it comes by design. It is this design which we try to provide.

We are concerned with establishing a pattern; with keeping costs under control and with maximum value for money; with identifying every aspect and every stage of the overall plan; with signposting potential pitfalls – in short, with providing a traveller's guide to exhibition country.

For the properly equipped it is richly rewarding territory. It needs planning, organisation and commitment. And once your objectives are clear, your budget settled and a responsible and enthusiastic Exhibit Manager chosen, your company is *en route* to all the benefits which flow from successful exhibiting.

In obedience to our own stated principle we must identify our 'target audience': we believe this book will be useful to everyone who participates in exhibitions, but we speak in the first place to those who have not yet entered this field, or whose experience of it is so far only occasional and irregular.

And once the innocent abroad (or at home) has taken the first step he will find hosts of people ready to help him. All who work in the exhibition industry have their own experience to offer in case he stumbles. Nobody wants him to fall. Their pride in doing a good job themselves makes his success their success.

After his first show, as he uses the exhibition medium more frequently, he will discover that it is like living in the market place. By listening with both ears, and speaking only half as much as he listens, he will discover that he has a hot line to the heart of the matter: an immediate knowledge of what the market needs and wants.

Part One

PLANNING YOUR EXHIBIT

1 Deciding to Exhibit

WHY EXHIBIT? Companies exhibit for a variety of reasons. Here are some of them:

1 Your company can display the full range of its products exactly as you want them; and you can make use of machinery, small or large, so that visitors can see what those products are capable of in operation.

2 The cost per visitor seen at an exhibition is very low, much lower than for any other means of advertising.

3 If you have a new product, showing it at an exhibition is an easy and extremely inexpensive way of launching it.

4 You can use the occasion for market research. An exhibition provides a good opportunity for testing the possible market for a new product by displaying a prototype and discussing its potential with people who come onto your stand. Among the visitors to your stand may be your competitors, but this is a risk well worth taking.

5 If you plan to go into a new market, an exhibition can be a very good way of penetrating that market, and many exhibitors planning to enter overseas markets follow this course.

6 The presence of the press will give you a ready-made chance of coverage in the media, whether television, radio or the trade press.

7 An exhibition offers a good opportunity to meet a large number of people important to you in a very short space of time.

8 Equally, an exhibition gives you a chance to talk in depth with anyone who comes to your stand.

9 Since many such visitors will be seeing your products for the very first time, you are thus increasing the potential market for your products.

10 Larger shows, especially international trade exhibitions, are likely to attract almost all the significant members of the purchasing public or trade in their field. Exhibiting gives you the chance to meet them.

11 Your technical and administrative staff also can meet visitors on your stand, something which does not ordinarily happen if your sales are entirely in the hands of representatives.

12 Most of the people who come onto your stand will do so not merely by

chance but because they are interested in something they have seen on it. This means that they will be already receptive to approach by your sales team.

13 But perhaps the most important reason for taking part in an exhibition and having your sales staff on your stand is that only here, in the exhibition hall, is the actual buyer on neutral ground. He can talk, and talk freely, to your sales people because he is not on your premises, nor you on his. This helps enormously, particularly for clients who are not ordinarily able to come and talk to you because of their links with your competitors or for other 'political' reasons.

Exhibiting may not always be the best answer to your needs. If, for instance, your only display material consists of text and photographs, then an exhibition may well be the last place to show it. Much better to send your potential clients a well designed and printed brochure with colour pictures and a personal letter.

Following through
You would do well to stay away from exhibitions, too, unless you are prepared to put in a great deal of hard work not only before but during and, importantly, after the exhibition itself. A common fault among exhibitors is that even though they apply a lot of money, effort and careful organisation to the production of their stand, they fail to carry that organising drive and salesmanship through to its proper conclusion, the object of the whole process.

Every stand within an exhibition must form part of an overall marketing strategy. The exhibition must not be allowed to finish on the show's closing day. You have to take up and pursue all the contacts you have gained. Only by thoroughly following this through will the exhibition really have done its job; otherwise you are unlikely to achieve the final object of your marketing strategy – more orders for your company.

The failure to follow through after the show has finished is probably the reason why, over the years, exhibitions have sometimes got themselves a bad name for failing to create new sales.

Exhibitions as a 'hands on' marketing medium are themselves fairly recent in folk memory. Many managing directors and senior decision makers have out-of-date memories of what constitutes an exhibition. To too many people it still means too much hard drinking, too many late nights, too many useless social events, too much money spent.

With proper planning there is no reason why this should be so. Exhibitions are ideal occasions for the sale of products, ideas and even techniques. They offer a chance to display objects to a very wide audience at a very low capital cost, and, over and above this, they provide a potential purchaser with an ideal opportunity to have a look at all the competing products available to him.

CHOOSING THE RIGHT EXHIBITION

Exhibition work is an aspect of advertising and promotion. Like all promotion you must decide – before you embark on it – what your objectives are. Unless you do this, you will have no yardstick for evaluating the results afterwards.

Ask yourself whether the exhibition really covers the market you need. Never decide to take part in an exhibition because you like the look of it, or of the hall it is being held in. However appealing it may all look, stay away unless the market is relevant.

Is it in the right place? It must attract the right audience, and it must be a suitable launch-pad for your new products.

And is it at the right time? It must fit in with your production schedules, and be capable of dovetailing with your other advertising and promotion. How do you actually find out if this is the right show for you? What sources will help you make your decision?

1 *The catalogue of previous shows*
This will give you a picture of what firms exhibited here in past years. A clue to their success or otherwise will be found in whether they are regular exhibitors, and whether they are showing again in the forthcoming exhibition.

2 *The Audience Certificate*
The kind of audience who came to previous exhibitions is harder to assess, but the better organisers are beginning to produce properly researched reports on the audience in the shape of Audience Certificates. They will be glad to give you this information; indeed it is often part of the publicity kit they send you when they try to persuade you to go into the forthcoming exhibition.

3 *Press reports*
Examination of the technical and trade press coverage of previous exhibitions will provide useful evidence to help you decide if in fact this is the right exhibition for you.

4 *'Eye-witness accounts'*
Information from the organisers naturally tries to persuade you to buy space at the exhibition. It will therefore have an element of bias. Try to find an independent source, perhaps someone who exhibited last time, or a client of yours who went to the show as a visitor; what did they personally think of it? Add their judgement to the evidence of the catalogue and the press, and you will be well placed to make the right decision.

But, remember again, participation is just an element in your overall marketing plans and, perhaps, of your wider plans for exhibiting at other exhibitions. Will there be duplication of effort? Are you going to appear in two different cities in similar exhibitions with similar audiences? Or can you choose instead two different kinds of exhibition which in giving you different audiences will increase the number getting your message? If so, can you use the same stand in both locations?

CHOOSING THE RIGHT SITE

How big should your site be?

A large company needs a large stand only if it intends to show large exhibits. A small stand, well designed and painstakingly produced, will often do a large company more good than a double-storey structure in the centre of the hall, as the latter may have nothing new to show.

Remember that up to half the visitors may have seen the exhibition last time. They do not want to see the same display again, however imposing. At the same time many visitors will of course be newcomers, so that a degree of repetition in the design (which will save costs) is permissible.

What is the best location?

Should your stand be near the entrance? On the main gangway? On a balcony perhaps? The visitors you want to get hold of will affect your choice. If you aim to attract everyone, perhaps you should choose a main gangway. But if you are after a specialised group of visitors, many of whom you will be inviting personally, then your stand could well be set back out of the mainstream. You will be able to conduct your business more easily if you are not interrupted by the random crowds milling through the exhibition.

You should also consider the location of your competitors. Do you really want to be opposite or next to your biggest competitor? The organiser can help you here. It is in his interest as well as yours that his exhibitors are happy with their location, for nothing is worse for him than to have exhibitors on opening day complaining that they are in the worst positions and unable to carry through their planned sales since the right people are simply not passing their particular stands. The organiser will be able to tell you, often at a quite early stage, exactly who is on the surrounding stands.

Remember, too, that if you have been participating for a number of years you can provisionally reserve your site for next time by pencilling in your name on the organiser's plan at the end of the previous exhibition. Indeed many organisers offer a discount if you sign and pay for next year at the end of the current show.

What type of site?

Most organisers can offer you anything from an island site (that is, one with gangways on all four sides) to a site with gangways on two sides, or on one side only. Your choice will depend on what you want to show and how you want to show it. Your designer's advice is important here, and you should involve him right from this earliest stage. He is likely to think that island sites are very difficult to present good displays on unless you are exhibiting heavy industrial machinery; and he will probably prefer a site with gangways on three sides, so that whichever way your visitors approach you a fully designed frontage will always face them.

SHELL SCHEMES

Nowadays organisers provide what is known as a Shell Scheme. This is a standard, usually modular, system of exhibition constructions grouped in a single range, each with its own walls, carpets and ceilings. The exhibitor has simply to provide the exhibits and the dressing within his particular framework or 'shell'. This is of course a cheap way of going into a major exhibition. You may not think it imposing or individual enough for your company, and may prefer to take space for your own special design on your own special stand. But the subject is worth a little more exploration.

Construction of the shell scheme is carried out by the contractors nominated by the exhibition organisers. Each stand within it is designed to a standard pattern and equipped with a number of basic features. Usually included are floor coverings (normally carpet tiles, which are widely used and efficient), signs to identify the exhibitor, lighting, and display items for product promotion, along with such basic equipment as tables, chairs and possibly shelves or display racks. An office or working area and general decorative aids may also be provided.

To this basis you can add a wide range of display fixtures and fittings, counter units and display panels of various sizes and colours. You can also incorporate purpose-built mountings for particular items or for prestigious settings framing star attractions.

Furnishing the stand, too, with your own choice of plinths (bases), office units, flower troughs, or electrical fittings, can add individuality. In the past exhibitors often objected to shell schemes as less attractive than specially designed stands. But recent improvements in their modular design and ancillary features have produced a versatility which means that no two stands need look alike. Your stand can now have such distinctiveness that the visitor will not even realise that the stand is just one of a standard range. His attention will be focused on what it contains.

They are not equally suitable for all products, but lend themselves particularly well to, for example, machines, foodstuffs, or textiles, whilst bathroom and kitchen equipment may be better shown on a purpose-built stand.

Their cost is often less than half that of an individual stand, and consequent savings may be large enough to allow the exhibiting group to participate in an additional show. Moreover, because of their standard layout, erection and assembly are faster than for a purpose-built stand. The time saved not only cuts down on building costs but also allows the exhibitor's representative to spend less time on site before the exhibition opens.

GROUP DISPLAYS – SEPARATE OR TOGETHER? Your company may be part of a conglomerate, with three or four other companies from the group exhibiting as well as your own. You have to decide whether you show all exhibits under a single banner on one large stand or whether each company should exhibit separately. The decision depends chiefly on the degree of sectionalisation in the exhibition and on the unity or disparateness of the constituent marketing teams. Experience suggests that it is usually better to exhibit as separate identities, with individual stands each in the right section of the exhibition, but with each underlining that it is part of the overall group and each referring to the locations of the others.

ORGANISING YOUR PARTICIPATION: THE EXHIBIT MANAGER

It is essential that right from the outset the participating organisation appoints one person with the overall responsibility for its exhibit and for all the planning and organising needed to fulfil its exhibition objectives. This person must be directly responsible to the Managing Director or someone of equivalent seniority; he must be seen to have top backing, for he will be taking decisions which will often have important effects on the image that the company puts before present and future customers.

He will not of course be on his own. The very nature of exhibiting means that very many others within the organisation will be involved; this is why the Exhibit Manager must be, and must be recognised as being, in charge of the whole programme. He oversees it from the first stage to the final evaluation, and throughout he will know precisely what is going on in every part of the total activity. He must be a full member of any committee involved, and must always attend. He represents the company, and the number of activities that have to be carried out and successfully co-ordinated within strict time schedules will probably mean it is not feasible for him to have any other major commitment during the entire period of the exhibition. He is the key to the success of the whole project.

THE GOLDEN RULES

There are ten golden rules which underpin any project, including the planning and execution of an exhibition display. The Exhibit Manager must:

1 agree objectives
2 establish command
3 allocate responsibilities
4 plan all dates backwards from opening (or 'D-Day')
5 give every divisional manager his own calendar
6 fix key meetings a long way in advance
7 circulate information reliably
8 chase progress relentlessly
9 check budgets regularly
10 resist afterthoughts ruthlessly

Success depends on adherence to these rules.

2 The Budget

This is the Exhibit Manager's first task. It has to be done before any designs are produced and indeed before many of the likely costs are known, but it is not impossible with the help of the checklist of necessary costings set out in Part Three.

Four major areas need to be taken into account:

1 Direct expenses

a) Space cost
Remember to note the actual dates on which specific payments for space have to be made to the organisers.

b) Shell scheme *or* custom-built stand
If you decide on a shell scheme, remember not to include costs for the basic structure which (unlike the custom-built stand) the scheme provides.

c) Stand fitting
There are three basic sections here:
Cost of display material
Cost of typography or graphics
Cost of models and specialist services such as lighting.

d) Additional services
Services you may need include electricity, gas, water and waste, compressed air, refrigerator, telephone and possibly telex, tickets and other publicity items provided by the organisers.

Check whether consumption of any of these is included in the stand price (and make a note to take meter readings at the start and at the end of the whole operation).

e) Insurance
There are a number of aspects to obtaining adequate insurance cover, some of them peculiar to exhibitions but mostly relating directly to your regular business. There is the obvious necessity to insure both your products and your staff when they are away from their regular base. Temporary cover at a recognised exhibition hall can best be obtained by getting your existing policy adapted through your broker; it should include travel and transportation both to and from the exhibition.

It is likely that your standfitting, furniture, lighting, flowers and special effects will all be hired through your stand contractor, and he can probably arrange for the insurance premium to be included in his final account.

In the unfortunate event that the exhibition itself is postponed, cancelled or open only for a part of its advertised time, you can take out a special contingency insurance to indemnify you against all your exhibition costs (and you should check too whether the organisers have their own contingency insurance which may cover part of your requirements).

This indemnity insurance can include the cost of buying space from the organisers, time and direct costs of building your stand, any special advertising you may have undertaken for your participation, and the cost of the outward and return journeys of your exhibits. This could be especially valuable for your peace of mind when the exhibition is in a different continent and the despatch time of your exhibit itself is several months before the event. For greater detail see separate insurance check list in Part Three.

f) Cleaning
Often, but not always, provided. Check the level provided and add extra costs if you need further work.

g) Furniture and carpets
These are usually hired, not bought, and must be returned in good condition.

h) Professional fees
By using designers, architects, or other professionals you will increase your stand's effectiveness and often relieve yourself of much worry. Involve the designer from the outset; he will provide very useful help in budgeting, and will carry out costings for production and for hidden costs such as VAT and insurance. Check whether he includes construction management in his costings.

i) Senior management visits
You must budget for a number of exhibition visits which may well include quite expensive entertainment and hotel costs.

j) Contingency
Write in a 15% contingency for all items not under your control or not fixed in advance.

2 Exhibit material

a) In-house exhibits
Make sure that the people responsible for providing these have co-ordinated lifting, packing and transport. And ensure that fixings are properly related so that you do not end up with pieces of your exhibit which do not fit together or have the wrong sizes, model numbers or colours.

It is well worth doing preliminary sub-assembly work before the component parts leave the factory, and packing them specially in order of assembly on site.

b) Bought-in items

Avoid manufacturers' specials; save money by using standard available pieces. Try to ensure, too, that decisions are made about bought-in items before going out to tender. Extras after the tender is accepted and contracts placed can prove exceedingly expensive.

c) Assembly

Allocate plenty of time for assembling and completing your exhibit. Make allowances for Murphy's Law.

d) Storage of exhibits

Your stand contractor can do this for you, but he will probably charge.

e) Testing exhibits

Carry out as much testing as possible at your own factory.

f) Transport

Schedule arrival times with the exhibition organiser for moving difficult, heavy or bulky items.

g) Lifting gear

Remember that you will have to take exhibits out after the exhibition ends as well as bringing them in at the beginning. Make sure your stand has easy access to goods entrances.

h) Contingency

If your budgeting for exhibit material is reasonably accurate, 10% should provide adequate contingency cover here.

3 Visitor promotion

a) Advertising: general

All aspects of advertising – press, radio, television, posters, point of sale and direct mail – must be considered. You can save a lot of money here by linking with and supplementing the organisers' own promotion and pinpointing your company in its particular relation to their general advertising.

b) Catalogue or buyers' guide: advertisements, extra copies, extra indices which cross-refer your exhibit

The catalogue has great potential for continuing use after the end of the exhibition. Major exhibitions take place only every two or three years and in the interval the catalogue can become a very important buyers' guide.

c) Technical press advertising

Your advertising agent must be involved from the start. Any advertisement you run in the months before the exhibition should incorporate the fact that you will be participating. This can be easily done by obtaining from the organisers the artwork of the exhibition logotype.

Consider also placing advertisements in any special industry supplements being produced for the exhibition. These supplements increasingly print detailed exhibition comments and critiques.

d) Technical Literature: design, artwork, blocks, printing, translation
Try to ensure that there is a visual link between your literature and your exhibit. You must decide on the numbers and quality of your brochures and other literature, and on the consequent cost.

Do they need to be produced also in languages other than English? Much of the content for the literature may already exist, but for the purpose of the exhibition it must be suitably designed to achieve your exhibition objectives and to support your exhibit.

You will also probably need brief literature about your company, your products and any key aspect like after-sales service or fixing details. This should be cheaply produced and given away freely to students, casual enquirers, marginally potential clients and competitors.

e) Public relations staff: fees and expenses
As with advertising, your public relations activities should be co-ordinated with those of the organisers. You can save a great deal of cost and effort by making use of what will undoubtedly be the large public relations drive which the organisers will provide.

f) *Ad hoc* entertaining: costs

g) Formal receptions: costs

h) Press releases: production and distribution: costs

i) Photography: costs
Suitable photographs for the press will be needed of your stand and particular elements of the exhibit; and also of important visitors to it.

j) VIP visitors
Once again, liaise with the organisers, but you will also have your own VIP visitors to bring, including head office and foreign buyers.

k) Special events
You may well decide that you are going to have competitions with prizes. If so, costs must be included in your budget.

l) Contingency
For visitor promotion a prudent contingency figure will be about 20%. This will allow you to take advantage of good ideas which may crop up later in the planning process.

4 Staff costs

a) Temporary demonstrators and receptionists

b) Permanent stand staff
The salesmen, reps and any others who are going to staff your stand must be trained. Among them should be someone with the specific responsibility of dealing with all press and photographer visitors. Do not charge salaries or office overheads against these staff costs.

c) Training courses
The Exhibit Manager should run short courses on the elements of

manning an exhibition stand. Add the cost of any longer courses your reps and salesmen may need to attend in advance of the exhibition.

d) The cost of films or videos

e) Briefing costs
Spend time getting the written staff brief right; and do not leave the actual briefing until opening day or you will miss a lot of valuable visitors.

f) Hotel costs
Satisfactory hotel accommodation is important, but it is simply for rest and relaxation, not for High Life. If a swimming pool or gymnasium is available so much the better. Fitness and health are essential during the long, exhausting exhibition hours.

g) Travel and car parking

h) Subsistence allowance

i) Security
This includes personal security as well as the security of the products you are exhibiting.

j) Passes, badges, staff uniforms
All these are helpful to your company and to visitors in identifying your personnel. Their turnout can be simple and casual provided it is smart.

k) Interpreters
These must be budgeted for if there is likely to be any foreign audience for your exhibit.

l) Contingency
Budget for a contingency of about 5%.

Overall budget summary
Whilst the foregoing outline budget guide, which attempts to cover all aspects of your exhibition participation, may appear long and detailed, not all the headings will be relevant in every case, and many of them will serve as a reminder rather than identify an exceptional cost. But if you follow this method in compiling your budget you should get close to the total likely costs.

COST YARDSTICK Like everything else the company does, there must be some cost yardstick for measuring success. For exhibitions this is relatively simple. Success can be measured by establishing the effective ratio of participation cost to the cost of each serious enquiry. This can then be easily compared with the cost of sending out a salesman to visit a possible customer. Research shows that the cost of an exhibition contact is only about one third of the cost of talking to someone in his own office. Remember again here that this takes no account of the special advantage that at an exhibition salesman and customer meet on neutral territory, nor of all the written references to your product that can be generated by the trade and technical press in their exhibition reviews.

THE SIXTY-STEP CHECKLIST

At this point you should make reference to the sixty step checklist (p. 127), and you will need to refer to it frequently and regularly from now on.

Your Exhibit Manager must be in full control throughout, and the list serves as a series of reminders to him on matters great and small. Who is to be given the responsibility for doing this? And that? And what deadlines must be met? Nobody is likely to forget to brief the designer or, probably, to organise transport or advertising. But what about the name board details? Getting the stand cleaned? Laying on a photographer? If the Exhibit Manager uses the checklist as his basis for organising (and allocating) every detail of each successive phase, he will be able to keep track of everything, and to keep control of everything, throughout the process. The result will be a successful exhibition.

PRE-CONDITIONS FOR SUCCESS

1 Your decision to exhibit must take into account (a) your total resources, financial and human; and (b) your total marketing mix over the next few months, which may be using any or all of TV, radio, trade press, direct mail, extra representatives.

2 It is untrue that the one-off exuberance of exhibitions does not warrant standard sober-sided organisational discipline. On the contrary, their many important advantages, dealt with in this book, make the detailed and exact planning which you would put into every other complex organisational activity more essential than ever.

3 Your staff can make or break your success. Only their full awareness of the exhibition's purposes, techniques and disciplines will turn your stand from an empty flag-showing exercise into a launching pad for projecting your company and its products towards new contacts, new customers and new markets.

THE UNIQUE BUYER/SELLER RELATIONSHIP

Exhibiting not only identifies you with your industry and provides a healthy meeting point with your competitors. It also provides unique opportunities for a direct and fruitful relationship with your buyers.

The buyers have left their place of work and come into the market place of their own free will. In doing so, they have left behind them all the daily pressures which ordinarily take so much of their time and energy. For once they are undistracted, so that – provided your stand attracts their notice – you will have their undivided attention.

The fact that they, the buyers, have freely come to you, the seller, will increase their receptiveness, and you must seize the psychological advantages which this reversal of the usual buyer/seller relationship offers. Just as a photographer in developing his film fixes the image to the best effect by a calculated combination of chemicals and fluids, so you, the exhibitor, must fix a lasting image in the memory of every potential buyer, an image which, imprinted in such favourable conditions, will readily recur in his mind at any time in the future. This fixing will make full use of the five human senses and not be visual only. The buyer will be able to handle the products and to enter into discussion about them with your staff; and out of these dialogues will come firm pointers for future decisions about product development.

Your unique selling and advertising position will pinpoint your customers for you and bring them to you face-to-face – many more of them than you could ever meet in a day of conventional sales calls. You will come into contact with customers whom you might not otherwise have met, and, provided you attract the right people, the cost of each interview will certainly be less and its effectiveness probably more than that of a traditional sales call.

SOME DRAWBACKS TO EXHIBITIONS

1 Exhibitions are expensive, and once committed it is difficult for you to withdraw.

2 As an exhibitor, you are substantially dependent for your success on the efforts of other people.

3 Exhibitions absorb large numbers of staff and often disrupt normal planning of your sales operation by removing your salesmen from their established locations for several days. Orders missed through conventional channels may have lasting effects.

4 There is a tendency to 'over-socialise' at exhibitions. Being constantly on show and ready at all times to greet anyone who wants to come aboard and discuss your product in detail can be physically debilitating.

5 Exhausted sales staff do not make the most effective envoys on your stand, especially since this may be the only chance the visitor has of seeing your corporate image. First impressions can so easily make or break a contract.

6 Company enthusiasm for the exhibition in its early stages may lead to a diffusion of objectives and subsequently to a sense of failure after the exhibition. Keep your colleagues in check beforehand and limit your objectives to achieve the best results.

Most of these drawbacks, however, can be countered by good planning and careful training.

3 Before the Brief is Written

THE MESSAGE AND ITS TRANSMISSION

What message do you want to get across? How best to do it? And what are the technical requirements for staging the products you want to exhibit? If you aim to carve a niche for yourself in a new market, you plainly need to make as many sales contacts as possible. This hard sell calls for exceedingly well displayed products and a salesforce well to the fore.

But if you aim primarily to show the flag, to remind old customers of your continuing presence, and particularly if you are a big conglomerate needing to leave no doubt that you are the leader in your field, then a different approach will serve. Your object will be the creation of a finely made and finished stand whose whole ambience must display the very highest quality; this will reflect the fact that you are out less to create on the spot new sales than to communicate an unmistakeable impression of already-achieved success.

YOUR STAND AS PUBLIC RELATIONS

Whichever of these two extreme positions, or whatever intermediate position, you take, the design and organisation of your stand will project an image of your company and of the products represented. Many of your visitors will be potential customers, some of them for the first time, and your stand design must convey an impression that helps to create sales. Its location, too – shell scheme or purpose built, against a wall or free-standing with two or more open sides, nearness to a main gangway – all these will affect its design.

WHAT TO SHOW

Never forget that it is the product, not the stand, which you are selling. The more brilliantly eye-catching the stand the better, for unless you attract visitors you are lost; but the stand must never detract from the central aim of telling as many people as possible about what you are selling, and telling them at a glance, without over-elaborate display jargon.

Wherever possible, put the product itself, not pictures of it, on display. Static displays are dull and unmemorable; demonstrate your products, how they function and what they do. If this is not feasible, take the greatest care to produce lively display boards with good coloured photographs and well-lettered captions legible from a distance. But wherever possible and however difficult to achieve, the products themselves should be on show. Words and pictures belong to brochures and advertisements, not to exhibition halls.

Of course you may need graphics, and your designer's expertise is essential if they are to make an impact. And you may want to consider the expense of mock-ups or models or audio-visual presentation, so that your visitors can see something more than they can get simply by reading your standard catalogues.

Showing too much is as ineffective as showing too little. Too many exhibits and too many messages will create confusion in the minds of your visitors. From the whole range of your products choose the ones likely to appeal, and sell, to visitors at this particular exhibition. If your current advertising is designed to promote a particular part of your range, link your display to those products. You may be producing a new range, in which case your stand will form a public launching-pad. Or perhaps you want to seek the reactions of some of your special visitors to the prototype of a potential development projected for production in a few months' time.

So there are many more reasons for going into an exhibition than simply to put your exhibits into the shop window for a quick sale. An overcrowded stand is likely to be an ineffective one, but specialist manufacturers – producers, say, of ironmongery – may want to display their entire range to establish that there is nothing they cannot provide. This will present your designer with a difficult and crucial task, for a chaotic display suggests a chaotic company. But a comprehensive display is the exception, and two basic principles remain: show actual objects, not words and pictures of them; and do not overwhelm your visitor by trying to show him too much.

THE ADMINISTRATION OF YOUR STAND

You will probably need an administrative core on your stand to serve as an office. There is merit in having this semi-open, so that visitors can see that it is a real business meeting room. Coats must be hung, the telephone (if there is one) properly located, the refreshments stored but ready to hand; the place for all these is in a small inner office with lockable cupboards, and your designer must incorporate this in his plan.

Furniture installed must harmonise with the overall design. But empty spaces should not be filled up with coffee tables and chairs, which not only restrict the visitor's movement but also encourage your staff to sit about, and create a generally crowded and messy appearance. Similarly, flowers must not obscure the exhibits or be there because they are obviously filling a design vacuum or as a blatant afterthought. Whether the designer or the Exhibit Manager takes care of these details, they are part of the planning and must not be left to chance.

YOUR STAND AS SALES PLATFORM

What do your staff need from the stand design to do their sales job effectively? How are they actually to make contact with the visitors? How many sales positions do you need and where should they be sited? The layout of the stand for this purpose, the number of sales staff at work at any one time, the way in which they are going to be working: these are all essential elements of the basic preplanning. Your designer needs very careful briefing here.

All too often the exhibitor gives very little thought to these elements, and he certainly cannot assume that his designer understands the selling process at exhibitions. Your marketing and sales department should advise on this aspect of the brief. They will know what your aim is in this particular exhibition. They will be fully aware, too, of the special sales advantage, discussed earlier, of meeting the client on neutral ground. Despite this advantage, however, the visitor still has to cross a psychological, if not a physical, barrier when he walks onto your stand, and this is the point at which the salesman's position and attitude are all-important.

Is he standing on the edge of the platform waiting to grab the passer-by and try to sell him something? Is he drinking coffee with his colleagues somewhere in the recesses of the stand, in a setting of such privacy that the visitor feels embarrassed to intrude? Either of these postures will put off a prospective client before a word has been spoken. The positioning of staff, it can be argued, is at least as important as the positioning of the exhibits themselves, and layout and circulation patterns must take account of them just as much as of display objects.

There is of course nothing to stop the visitor from absorbing a great deal of time in discussing the products and then sauntering away without any indication of his intentions, if any. But all enquiries must be recorded, as described on pp. 35–6, and training of your sales staff will have taught them to winnow out the merely idle enquiry. But it will have taught them something equally important, that willingness to spend time with visitors, even apparently unpromising ones, may lead to useful orders in the fullness of time. They will recall hearing about the architectural student who asked at two different stands at a large building exhibition about a roofing product relevant to his project at college. The first in effect rebuffed him; the second put in time and effort in helping him solve the problems of his project. Years later, now a successful architect with a large practice, it was not surprising that he tended regularly to make use of the roofing products of the second firm he had visited at the outset of his career.

ATTRACTING ATTENTION TO YOUR STAND

Most people will view your stand in three stages.

First, they will see it from a long way off, at the end of a gangway or from the gallery looking out across the whole exhibition hall. This first point of communication calls for some visual sign which will locate and fix the stand for them.

Second, as they get closer, the crowd in the gangway will effectively stop them from seeing any detail of the stand. Perhaps the only thing clearly visible will be the upper or fascia part. This is the part which needs easily recognisable corporate identity signs, so that they will appreciate that they are passing your particular stand or, if they are intentionally looking for it, that they have found it.

Third, once they are walking alongside your stand and looking into it, there must be something to catch their eye and stop them in their tracks, in the face of all the other distractions.

Eyecatchers

Care must be taken with eyecatchers. They mustn't simply catch the eye, but must have a relevance to the product you are selling. A pretty girl perched on a piece of machinery, a method often used in the past, would certainly catch the eye of male visitors, but it would by no means follow that their eye would move on to any examination of the product. There is a widespread feeling among those well-versed in exhibition marketing and sales that using a pretty girl in this way is often the last resort of the PR or advertising man who can't think of anything better.

Far more sensible is to have a display related to your product. It may even be made out of your product so that the visitor cannot fail to connect what he is seeing with what you are selling. Early trade shows had a regular method of display which was known as 'Trophy'. This comprised the gathering together of a large number of products, not always the same one, into a massive decorative shape (sometimes quite exotic, such as a mountain of Californian walnuts moulded into the form of an elephant). The method is little employed nowadays, but imaginatively used it could still provide an effective eyecatcher.

It is sometimes said that much modern exhibition design is so architectural in form that the basic product display becomes quite secondary. Are you really looking – and you may be – for a stand which is a great architectural monument with perhaps two or three of your products dispersed on it? Your designer and you must carefully explore and agree on the balance of these two elements when decisions are being made at the outset.

CHOOSING YOUR DESIGNER Whoever is to design your stand will need a full written brief. By the time you prepare it you will already have settled a number of preliminary points.

1 Why have you chosen to go to this particular exhibition? What do you hope to achieve by it?

2 Is your aim a hard sell or a suitable environment in which to entertain existing and potential customers?

3 Is your participation to be tied in with an already existing advertising campaign?

4 Have you already booked your space? If so, your designer must have full information, including services, physical limitations, position of aisles, likely flow pattern of visitors, and an overall plan of the entire exhibition hall layout.

5 He will also need full information on your company and its entire range of products, not just those planned for display at this exhibition. Written information must include the detailed requirements of your proposed

exhibits: their weight, dimensions, fire risk, safety requirements, the need for electricity, water, compressed air, gas and other services. He needs to know these things not only to create an effective working stand but also to plan efficient visitor access, and entry and exit for the exhibits themselves. Notes on your competitors and their products, especially if they are likely to be at the same exhibition, will help him too.

Sources for the choice of designer

1 *In-house design.* You may already have an in-house design division, but beware: even if your top draughtsman is used to dealing with your products he may have no experience of exhibition design and so be quite the wrong person for this specialised and complex task. If you do use him, his existing workload must at once become a secondary priority, but there remains a risk that he will gear his work, if only subconsciously, to what he knows management will accept rather than to what the market needs.

2 *Independent designers.* You may already be using a firm of independent designers to manage your corporate identity programme, to design your new products or to work with your advertising agency on your continuing programmes. In this case you should see if they can also provide you with your stand design needs. Nevertheless they should be closely examined to evaluate their special skills in the instant and up-to-the-minute world of exhibitions, which demands speed rather than perfection.

There are a number of freelance designers who spend much of their lives on this kind of work, and this is the prime field in which you are likely to find your answer. But you must choose the right person with the right experience. It is essential that you see a portfolio of his work, and equally essential that in talking with him you find out whether he is likely to get on with you and your staff. You should talk also to people who have used him before. Most freelance designers will be only too happy to put you in touch with previous clients so that you can get first-hand evidence on what it is like to work with them and whether they are dependable in completing projects on time and keeping within specified budgets.

Note that whilst very few advertising agents or public relations companies have exhibition designers actually on their staffs they may well be able to give you advice about the selection of an independent designer.

3 *Stand-fitting companies.* Many of these have in-house designers. But a word of warning: unless your brief is crystal-clear you will be in danger of getting what is ideal, not for your purpose, but for the purpose of the stand contractor. He will have already to hand various items of display equipment and structure which he will be keen to make use of, and you may well emerge with a stand which is far from ideal for your own purpose.

4 *Amateurs.* The one thing you must on no account do is to give the job to your talented son who happens to be in the second year at his school of architecture – or to your niece who is rather good at picking colour schemes for her front living room. They may very well have flair, but the likelihood of their producing a stand which is going to be any use to you is

negligible; and never allow the Chairman's wife anywhere near the project!

You may well decide to choose an independent designer. If he is the right man for the job he is likely to find exhibition work a particularly exciting medium. Its temporary nature allows new ideas to be tried out and creativity to be given its head; after all, even if it is not 100% successful it will not be there for long. A good designer will not allow his creativity to be impaired by the constraints of the brief and the surrounding regulations. It is often the really difficult site and brief which produces the most striking and memorable results; good designers don't like to be beaten. But just because he is a creative person you will need to check his work right through the design process to make certain he is keeping to the brief and not embarking on any flights of fancy, perhaps encouraged by your sales staff.

Most designers offer a service covering the whole process of design, tendering and construction supervision. As to fees, these are usually charged as a percentage of the actual production cost or, should you prefer it, they will quote you an hourly rate.

COPING WITH CRISIS

A prime reason for your choice of the exhibition medium is to be able to show potential buyers the products themselves. But there is always a risk, particularly with new products, that they may be held up in production or not tested or approved in time.

Weeks – or even hours – before the exhibition opens you may have a large empty space on your stand. You must have contingency plans:

● your furniture supplier may be able to let you have more items simply to fill the gap and provide at least a meeting area where you can sit and talk to potential customers

● your local stockists or agents may have goods in their stockroom which will help you fill the space

● a large customer who has recently taken delivery of some of your equipment may be willing to lend it for the duration of the exhibition

● if he cannot do this, he may be prepared to let you take small parties of really interested customers out to his factory to see the equipment in operation

● if the exhibition is overseas there is a similar possibility of borrowing something either from stockists or from customers in neighbouring countries and airfreighting it in

● if these courses are not feasible you must increase the manning of your stand so that at least people familiar with the product and armed with brochures are on hand to talk with visitors. Again, your local agent may be able to second some of his own salesmen to you

● you are not bound to apologise. If there has been a shipping breakdown, a fire or some other disaster, don't hide it. Tell the story (making use here of the organisers' daily news sheet), and you may be surprised to find how many others have been in some similar predicament

● if the crisis occurs overseas, check on and exploit local customs and provide extra space for the statutory tea drinking in the Middle East, the serving of cold tea in Indonesia or a tea ceremony in Japan

● an overseas crisis makes it not only important but imperative that you have really good local interpreters. Your local agent should be able to provide you with a choice

● if some of your products are missing, the staff on your stand will need to be even more alert and positive. You may have to extend their stay at the exhibition so that visitors can be taken round to see your machinery operating under local manufacturing conditions

● emergency graphics may be called for. If so, make sure that they show your machines working locally, and give full credit – pictorial coverage, names and addresses – to any firms allowing you to visit them

● a useful failsafe in your initial planning is the preparation of hand-carried items such as slides and video tapes. These may save the day in a crisis, and will help to convey the impression of an active and busy stand.

DEALING WITH LARGE EXHIBITS

Liaise from the outset with the organisers if your exhibits have any special requirements. They may need, for instance, particular electrical supplies, and the organisers will probably have explicit instructions here. Machinery which uses a great deal of power will have to be switched on at the start of each day, and the organisers will certainly stipulate varying times for the controlled use of power so as to make sure that the whole system for the Hall does not overload at once and plunge the show into darkness.

If you intend to use large, heavy or awkward-shaped exhibits you must programme their delivery early on with the organisers. You will not be allowed to try craning them in at the last minute when the aisles are already clogged by other contractors working on their stands. Again, floor loadings must be checked. A lot of exhibition stands, especially in Europe, are built of wooden platforming, and this will collapse under very heavy weights unless you take suitable steps. The usual course is to lay bricks under the platform to carry the load straight down to the structural floor of the hall, and this must of course be done right away. This reinforcement is necessary right along the route the exhibit will take as it is manhandled to its final position.

Forward planning in collaboration with the organisers is once again essential. In fact, with heavy exhibits, the late arrival of exhibits or any other problems, the organisers are likely to be your best ally. As your objective is an effective and successful stand, so theirs is an effective and successful exhibition.

Exhibitions are celebrations. Fully fledged flagpoles with international flags lend authority to the event.

If the airspace above your stand can be used effectively with a message, make use of it.

Information stands, well designed, and the staff with cheerful faces and a strong corporate dress sense.

If you're not ready on time, try to keep the workmen out of sight when the public are in the building.

It's all right to use your own stand for directional signs and footprints but be cautious about using a common gangway.

It is nice to be welcomed by everyone on the stand when you arrive, but make sure that visitors are also allowed on and not defensively kept away.

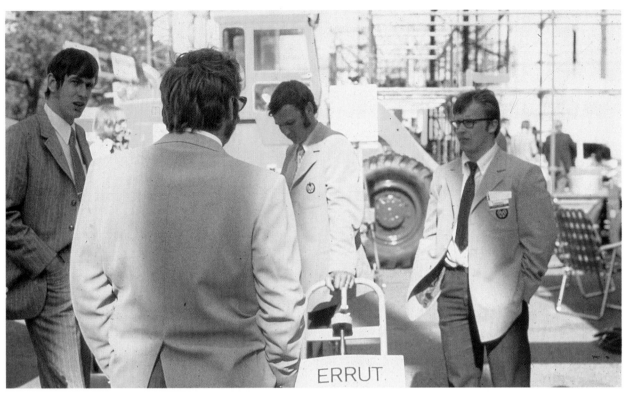

It is important to distinguish members of exhibitor staff from visitors, and the use of the same coloured jackets achieves this very successfully.

An excellent example of a designer knowing that people need to rest their eyes by changing focus. The ability to look through the stand and then back onto the sign is an excellent design bonus.

A NEW product, but new to whom? Even people a long time in the industry don't know everything that is available. But NEW is always an attractive word.

Plenty to read, but no message for the visitor doing a quick walk around.

RIGHT *It is good to see those chairs ready for a presentation, but how do you get onto the stand?*

ABOVE *Corners of stands are always difficult to treat; this makes it clear that access is available but it may be disconcerting if you are trying to walk backwards off the stand.*

RIGHT *All the chairs have their backs to the gangway, so that anyone sitting in them would have the top of his head exposed to passing visitors. And also, how do you get onto the stand?*

LEFT *This stand has been designed so that the visitor may step off the gangway onto the stand in order to look at the products, but the ankle-height captions and exhibits do make it difficult to get into conversation with an exhibitor.*

If you want to offer advertising carrier bags, make them freely available to visitors. Don't expect your visitor to kneel down in order to pick up a leaflet from the floor.

Chairs clearly invite people to stop and be entertained but it is very difficult to keep such an area clean, tidy and welcoming.

The flowers under this board do add a visual dimension to the stand and give a more welcoming look.

LEFT   The flowers add nothing to the wall of the stand and the milk crate should have been removed before the exhibition opened.

A workaday machine can be enhanced by flowers but don't enclose it so that visitors can't get to and examine the controls.

ABOVE LEFT *This appears to be a special offer for the exhibition but is not given prominence, and it might be difficult to follow up.*

ABOVE *There are no captions on these products and the space above eye level is ideally suited for describing the company or its products. Flowers underneath tidy up the whole effect and enable the reverse side of the stand to be used without being seen from the gangway.*

A good example showing how flowers can bring into stark relief the design of the surrounding hard-edge products.

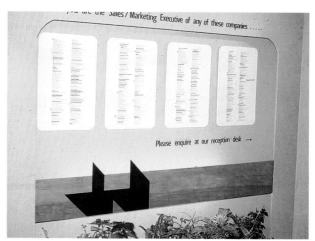

ABOVE LEFT   *The hard edges of illuminated walls or side panels can usually be softened by the use of a tree, which enhances the general effect.*

ABOVE   *Two simple words say everything about the product – the letters are large enough to be seen from a distance and are at the correct height to be seen by the fast track visitor. The use of a tree with minimum foliage softens the look and draws attention to the words.*

LEFT AND BELOW   *The panels in these two photographs have an important message for every visitor. People are intrigued to see if their own names appear on a list and will usually want to spend a minute looking for themselves and seeing who else is on it. Secondly, being able to cross off names of people seen during the week heightens the interest of the panel and makes it even more likely that the remainder of the names will eventually find their way to the stand before the show closes.*

4 The Catalogue and the Press

Exhibitions are by their nature ephemeral things and the catalogue forms the only permanent record. In time it will provide the historian with a lasting indication of the state of the industry at any one stage; and, of more immediate importance, it continues, in the case of large international exhibitions, to be a chief source of information for buyers right through until the next exhibition, which may be as much as five years away. In other words, a properly prepared entry will give you – and the entry is usually free – up to five years' publicity. So make full use of it.

A surprising number of exhibitors fail to do this. It is extraordinary that they are prepared to spend a very large sum of money on exhibiting but take very little trouble indeed to capitalise on it by linking their exhibiting to an overall selling campaign which exploits the catalogue, and associates it with an advertising and press exercise. Two months before a recent food exhibition which had some 600 exhibitors, only 72 had provided the organisers with catalogue information; indeed, one of them, already contacted eight times by phone and telex, was still returning the message that the organisers should, they hoped, be getting the information by the end of the following week. This was either bad organisation or a sign that the Exhibit Manager had too little authority (or too much scope for interference). And occasionally there have even been exhibitors who have declined to appear in the catalogue at all, claiming that they wanted to retain 'a low profile'. Any company aiming at a profile as low as that probably shouldn't be in the exhibition at all.

The organiser will send you a sheet on which to fill in your standard entry, and may ask you also to choose the classified product indices you want to be included under. Remember to be comprehensive rather than cursory in completing the latter, and return them both as soon as you possibly can. Take pains with this task, which need not be daunting provided you have a written statement of your objectives. But if there are real problems, then at least get some general information, including your factory telephone number and telex, into that vital and long-lasting publication. And if you are planning, as part of your current advertising campaign, to take advertising space in the catalogue as well, the organiser can be a great help to you in displaying your advertisement to the best effect and in the right place. Do not throw away the advantages the catalogue offers, or jeopardise the organiser's good will by leaving him to pursue you repeatedly for basic entry information.

There are other reasons for getting your entry to the organiser in good time. He is fairly certain to print the whole catalogue at once. If you miss this printing your entry will appear only on those addendum sheets which end up strewing the floor of the Hall, or falling out of your client's copy — and even if it survives these hazards he is unlikely to remember to look at it. If you *have* met your deadlines you can often get the organiser to let you have advance copies of the catalogue to send to the really important people you want to come to the exhibition.

THE PRESS

Press publicity

The catalogue is just one of the sources of publicity which, all too often, are neglected. Many companies, sometimes quite large ones, are bad at taking advantage of the whole system of publicity which the organisers can offer, apparently thinking that by taking space for their stand they are at the same time having their publicity organised for them. They will be disappointed. The organisers are closest to the press since they have already been through the process of publicising the exhibition to visitors; in doing so they will have certainly talked to the specialist trade editors. But both organisers and press are sure to be starved of information from most of the exhibitors.

It is a fallacy that the press will be pestering the exhibitor. The less they have to do this the better they will like it. Their task is quite difficult enough already. They will not be totally familiar with every sector of your particular company (and all the others as well). But they are expected to write, collate, edit and publish, at high speed, articles on all the latest developments in the industry. Needing all the help they can get, they like to be offered information rather than to slog round searching it out for themselves.

Press kit

The information they are offered must be carefully organised. Put a kit together for the press, and make sure it includes really well-taken photographs and beautifully drawn diagrams showing, perhaps, cross-sections of your machinery or views of the stand hard to get in the jostle of the exhibition hall itself. And make certain you always have enough copies of the kit. It may well be that later in the exhibition a journal will send a reporter back as it is running a separate article on products of which yours form part. Keep enough kits at hand to last for the whole exhibition. Your publicity manager will probably be on the stand on press day, but you will do well to nominate a key staff member to be responsible for press kits and for dealing with journalists during the rest of the exhibition.

Press preview

Six months or so before the exhibition the organisers will tell you of any trade journals planning previews. Many of your potential visitors will be looking at these previews and will very likely be influenced by them in deciding what they particularly want to see. So send the editors information about your proposed exhibits; don't wait to be asked for it. The consequent publicity is free. They will no doubt try to persuade you to take out advertising space to complement their text. But the chances are that if you have good and interesting products they will cover them, regardless of whether or not you are advertising in that issue. Here again pictures are of the highest importance, since they will save the journals from having to send their own photographers round. Good artists' impressions of the stand, or photographs of the stand model, have an excellent chance of being published in technical press exhibition previews.

In the case of a major international exhibition an entire issue may be given over to a preview. It is imperative that you do all you can not to be left out – as you will be if you don't take the trouble to send the information to the editor. Failures on the press side usually result from not having one single person clearly in charge of press, public relations and marketing strategy over the whole exhibition period. Make certain you don't run the risk of this failure.

SUPPORTING PUBLICITY

For your important prospects you can obtain from the organisers invitation tickets overprinted with your firm's name and stand number. This costs you very little and will give your client reduced price or free entry and a clear destination within the exhibition hall. If such people are coming at specific times, keep an appointments book on the stand so that high calibre staff are on hand when they come. And if your company maintains some form of card index or listing of all contacts, either have a copy on the stand or a computer terminal on line to head office, so that you can call up the information and avoid the embarrassment of finding, just as he is leaving, that the visitor you have been chatting to is in fact one of your most important clients.

Most of the larger exhibitions hold a number of seminars and other meetings as part of the programme. Try to arrange for someone from your staff to talk or participate, and invite some of your clients to come as well.

On a lesser plane, giveaways – carrier bags for exhibition literature, balloons, lapel stickers, keyrings, or miniature products – are often welcomed as souvenirs. Even managing directors of large companies may have small children at home, and it can hardly fail to nudge their memories if they see their youngest running about in a tee-shirt emblazoned with the name of your company.

RECORDING ENQUIRIES

All exhibition enquiries must be promptly and properly recorded, and systematically followed up by your local agent or by whoever normally deals with sales enquiries at head office. Nothing will ruin your reputation more effectively than simply filing and forgetting enquiries. It often happens that some of the enquiries are made only out of general interest at the time. But if you follow them up in a businesslike way with your catalogue this will count in your favour should the enquirer, months later, have a specific need for your product and have to decide between you and your competitors for supplying his need.

Enquiries can be properly recorded only by adequately briefed staff. This will not happen if you follow the familiar practice of hiring a number of decorative people to look after your stand. Even with an afternoon's briefing they will have, at best, very little knowledge of your products. At regional exhibitions, at home or abroad, use your regional staff; their knowledge of local conditions makes them the obvious people to follow up local enquiries. In any event there must always be someone on your stand who knows your products inside out, so that when the visitors arrive (and among them, perhaps entirely unexpected, may be one who is vitally important) you can depend on their being met by an informed representative of the company who will record their queries sensibly and ensure that they are followed up. And it is worth stressing once more that an adequate supply of trade and publicity literature must always be available. There is no excuse for failure here.

5 Exhibiting Overseas

REPRESENTATION If you have no established local agent already, the exhibition gives you an opportunity to find one. Ask about possible people at the commercial department of your embassy or consulate, and do this several months before the exhibition takes place so that you may meet them during the exhibition and talk over the possibility of their becoming your regular representative; they in turn can use the opportunity to have a look at your company and its products on display. Indeed, many companies initially exhibit in a country with the primary object of establishing suitable permanent representation in that country. But even for this initial exhibition you will need a man on the spot to steer you through the pitfalls of language, local laws, customs and business methods, and a great deal else besides. Help will be available too from the local exhibition organiser, who here as elsewhere has as his aim maximising the benefits to you and to himself of your participation.

TRANSLATION Your agent must have a real command of English, spoken and written, as well as of the local tongue. Outside the English-speaking world you will of course have to rely on commercial translation of your trade literature and publicity material. Your agent will be able to check that this is sharply practical rather than flowery, that it is accurate, and that it avoids laughable or offensive mistakes, which might well damage your chances of local sales. Equally he can make sure that your literature does not, even inadvertently, use unsuitable pictorial material, a factor specially to be watched for in different cultural milieux like the Middle or Far East.

You will also need an interpreter on the stand itself. Your agent can help you find one and, if he takes the task on himself, may well know or recognise important visitors and be able to help you make direct contact with them.

Your agent can get you much better local press coverage than anyone back at home could achieve. He is likely to know personally the editors of local papers and journals and will probably be familiar with their particular style of writing and presentation. If so, he may be able to place articles, written by himself in a suitable way, in the local press.

LOCAL LAWS, CUSTOMS AND BUSINESS METHODS These will certainly cause you worries the first time you exhibit in a country, and they may even get you into serious trouble unless your agent pilots you through them. Remember too that if you have not yet got an agent the exhibition organiser and very probably the local consulate, through its trade consul, will know more about local law and business methods than you are ever likely to find out on your own.

THE SITE Before you even get to the exhibition you should check the nature of the site with the help of your agent or the organiser. The designer will need to know about environmental factors like high humidity, great heat or unusually variable daily temperature changes. And any requirements for special services will need ordering several months earlier for overseas than for home exhibitions.

Electricity voltage and cycles (which may well be quite different from those at home) must be right. You may need to ship in special transformers, and these take time to obtain. Telephones may also present difficulties; the hall may not have facilities for temporary lines for direct connection to individual stands. And some communication systems may not be available at all, so that if you are looking for telex or computer modems and the like, you must talk to the organisers, to your local consulate and possibly to the country's national suppliers of phone, telex, telefax and similar services. To repeat: all these aspects of the proposed site must be checked at the outset and work put in hand at once.

TRANSPORT Nowadays a lot of exhibition material will be sent in by air or road, but larger exhibits still have to go by sea because of their weight or size. There is very much less merchant shipping nowadays than there used to be, and shipping arrangements must be booked very early indeed. Allow plenty of time too for comprehensive documentation, packing and crating. Indeed your delivery dates should make allowance for the worst – for strikes, storms and other hold-ups beyond your control.

Ask the exhibition organiser if there is an appointed shipping agent for your country. He may already be gathering exhibits from other companies; if so, you can obtain the benefit of groupage rates or of sharing the costs of the same container.

Is the site in a bonded customs area? If so, a plethora of form filling will be called for before you can take your exhibits in at all. Check all this, and check, too, the nature of the unloading facilities. Don't, in short, send off your material and hope for the best. Think about fallback positions before you start off, for you can often take some materials with you on the plane. They are much more easily come by at home in your own factory than in the country where the exhibition is taking place.

INSURANCE In the ordinary way you will probably yourself insure your stand and its contents, the exhibits, bought-in exhibit material, rented items and personnel, as discussed on p. 19. But if all these are going to be transported great distances to an overseas exhibition then the situation is different. You will need to discuss things with specialist insurance companies, and in circumstances involving any unusual risk your broker should refer the matter to a Lloyds insurance broker specialising in contingency risks who will place your insurance specially in the Room at Lloyds. In the USA and elsewhere you should contact an insurance broker with a Lloyds of London connexion in order to take advantage of the worldwide contingency rates that are available through London.

MONEY Needless to say, money overseas and its accessibility is a highly important matter. At home you may be used to saying, 'please invoice me' and clearing the account at the end of the month. Abroad you may not even be allowed out of the exhibition or onto the plane home until you have actually paid all local bills. So you are going to need quite a lot of ready money, and this can be organised in various ways.

Your home bank can arrange for you to have a cheque-cashing agreement with the nearest exhibition branch of one of the banks, in the exhibition hall in the country where the exhibition is being held. This is one of the safer ways of making certain that money is readily available to you overseas, but there are snags. Many people abroad are unwilling to accept cheques, and insist on hard cash. And although few countries will restrict the sum you can take in, some have regulations about the amount you can take out. You must therefore take care not to end up with a credit balance which you cannot retrieve at the end of the exhibition. Your bankers are the best source of advice; they will be able to tell you all about the regulations for taking your money in and out of any country. In any event, make sure that your budget designates the currency for each item of expenditure, and that all concerned agree to accept payment in the currency you nominate.

Personal costs for you and your staff – hotels, travelling, food and the like – are best paid by the use of credit cards or by taking the money in the form of travellers' cheques. Unless you can get a considerable discount for payment in cash it is unwise to carry a great deal with you. Thefts from hotel rooms, luggage or even pockets are considerable and for those people who insist on cash payment you would do well to invest in a money belt or similar means of keeping your cash out of the sight and reach of petty criminals.

In many countries tipping is still a fact of life and the only way to ensure action. At home it would be startling to find that we could not get an exhibit moved from lorry to exhibition hall without tipping someone to do it; but in some countries it is a normal and necessary procedure to pay for services like this on top of the quoted fee. TIP is said to stand for 'To Insure Promptness', so make sure that the tip equates with the service supplied. Indeed there are places where it is said to be necessary to tip airline staff to accept your baggage and clear your ticket so that you can board the plane at all. These things sound daunting until you have actually experienced them; but again the local exhibition organiser and your commercial consul will be able to advise and forewarn you.

COPYRIGHT   You must make certain that your prized exhibits have proper copyright protection. There are countries where you may proudly exhibit your latest product, make perhaps two or three sales, and discover two years later that there are now eight companies in the country where the exhibition was held that are producing identical products. If your product is copyrighted or design-registered or otherwise protected by patents, make sure that the country in which you intend to exhibit has properly guaranteed standards of protection. Exhibitions registered with UFI or other international organisations normally have guaranteed minimum standards in this area; but check beforehand.

KINDS OF EXHIBITION   You will need to establish the quality of competition and the local standards of presentation so as to discover the level at which you should pitch your stand. Don't (to put it crudely) turn up with a double-decker stand in a hall where everyone else is just using curtains on rods and a few scattered carpet tiles. The organiser will be able to tell you about design levels and probably provide you with photographs of previous exhibitions which will give you an idea of what to expect.

WORKMANSHIP OVERSEAS   Do you bring your own contractor with you or do you allow a local contractor to build your stand? Your decision will be made in the light of likely costs but also in the light of the standard of workmanship you may expect. The decision may of course be taken for you if your own contractor is not allowed to work in a particular country or exhibition hall. But local standards will sometimes surprise you, given the tools and equipment used. In Japan, for instance, your carpenter may arrive with just a simple tool bag but his craftsmanship may be at least the equal of anything you are likely to encounter at home, and many Far Eastern countries produce exceedingly well built stands. But when you are abroad, it is worth looking at standards in adjacent countries. They may have a much better contracting industry than anything in the country of exhibition. This industry may already be well used to taking exhibits across the frontier, and even be already working at your intended exhibition because the country in question does not have its own exhibition resources.

'SUITCASE DISPLAYS'   In a foreign country, especially where you are without a local agent whose offices you can use, you may well need to organise rooms for business in the exhibition grounds or in a local hotel. But do you in fact always need the full panoply of a large-scale stand? The show may be quite a small one; indeed, it may be a hotel show using bedroom facilities as the exhibition area. If so, think about assembling one of the sophisticated suitcase exhibition displays so often used in North America in certain industries such as consumer goods or clothing, where fashion designs must be concealed from the gaze of casual onlookers, competitors and copyists alike. These suitcase stands are usually simple tube and panel structures which fold up into a specially designed case and can be airfreighted with you in your plane, taken straight to your hotel room and set up in half an hour. They save a lot of money and, together with the existing facilities of a hotel show, tables, chairs and basic lighting, can provide you with all you need.

VISITORS   If you are exhibiting in an area where you have no sales staff or showroom, you may want to seize the golden opportunity to fly in special or prospective clients. Don't just post them an invitation; bring them in on a personal visit. Of course they will look at the rest of the exhibition as well, but if they are there at your invitation and expense they will put in a lot more time on your stand than elsewhere.

6 Staff Selection and Training

A number of references have already been made to staff – to their selection, training, appearance and roles. The present section, which considers all aspects of exhibition staff, here and there repeats points already made, and does so deliberately. For without a fully effective staff the whole enterprise is at risk and probably doomed. Military commanders who plan a jungle campaign organise supplies, arrange transport, set up communications, and ensure contingency reinforcements and replacements. It would be unthinkable if they didn't also brief the men who will be doing the fighting and train them in the techniques of jungle warfare. But companies setting out to participate in exhibitions will, all too often, devote immense care to planning the campaign but totally fail to provide proper training and briefing to the front-line troops who will be manning the stand. They will be heading for defeat.

Whether your stand is manned by your regular full-time employees or by people brought in specially to help your senior sales manager, they must know what they are doing, how they should do it and why. Uppermost in their minds must be the realization that there will usually be four main aims: making direct sales; recording hard business enquiries; making appointments to call on visitors after the exhibition ends; and obtaining the names and addresses of all the visitors they might otherwise not have met.

HOW MANY STAFF?

Too many staff (crowding out a small shell-scheme stand, chatting, brewing up and reading the job ads in the paper to pass the time) are as bad as too few. If you have exhibited before, the kind of product you are selling and the kind of client you are selling it to will help you to assess the number of staff needed. But even if this is your first exhibition, you should already have decided at the planning stage, and briefed your designer accordingly, on how many sales points you will have and what sales methods you will use. A useful question to ask yourself in checking (in both senses) your staff numbers is: if I plan to have this or that number of staff on my stand, what is each of them actually going to be doing? Selling highly complex technical equipment to a highly technical clientele will need your own experts on hand throughout. Selling to a general clientele can be done by two or three of your responsible people with temporary exhibition demonstrators. But the latter must know your objectives, your product and what you require from them.

THE RIGHT STAFF   Whether temporary or regular employees, the stand staff will need to be presentable, to have the right attitude, and to have adequate stamina. They are going to be out front, representing your company. They must be well turned out, enthusiastic and helpful – and they must know not only about your product but also where the toilets, phones and restaurants are. If the exhibition is abroad you must decide whether they need languages other than English (and if so, how many of them), and if the exhibition is any distance from your home base you will of course have to arrange travel and accommodation for them. At no time must the stand be left unattended. A really well organised staff rota, which always keeps a minimum of senior people on duty, and allows for sickness, is imperative. Duty stretches should not be longer than three hours, followed by a break of at least half an hour.

STAFF TRAINING   You may be demonstrating a production process. If so, the demonstrator will do his task differently from the way he does it in the factory, more slowly and deliberately and explaining as he goes along. But whatever kinds of activity take place on the stand, staff must be trained, and that training must make clear to them that working in the no-man's-land of an exhibition hall is very different from knocking on a client's office door; normal sales sequences may need rethinking, modifying or abbreviating. Give staff a written brief, and don't leave it until the end when everything will probably be running late.

STAFF BRIEFING   The following questions should be addressed in the written brief:

1 What will the stand feature?

2 What new products will be shown?

3 What special displays will there be?

4 Who is manning the stand? Who are the specialists? Who are the senior staff?

5 What is the geography of the stand? (i.e. Where do you hang your coat? Visitors' coats? Where are the phones?)

6 What are the phone numbers of the organisers? Of the maintenance staff for audio-visual equipment? And of the stand fitters for repair or replacement?

7 Who do you phone if the electricity fails?

8 What do you do if the phone itself fails? In short, provide a list of everyone involved, so that help is never more than a phone call away.

9 What are the home phone numbers for the Managing Director and the Sales Director in case you suddenly hear of a VIP visit due the next day?

10 Where are the drinks kept, and what is the policy for giving drinks and refreshments?

11 What is the policy for handing out your more costly brochures? Or do you only distribute them by appointment after the exhibition?

12 What is the geography of the hall itself? Where are the public phones, the banks, the refreshments, the organisers' office, the stairs, the lifts, the press office, the lost property, the first aid, the toilets? And the way home?

If your staff are to operate efficiently, they need all this information in a handy folder; and there must be enough copies to cover the rota for the duration of the exhibition. Make sure that replacement staff and visitors from head office also know the facts.

SMARTNESS

Staff must be smartly and comfortably dressed. They should avoid batteries of ballpoints in the breast pocket, and avoid new shoes also, for standing all day is an exhausting business. A good night's sleep is essential; fatigue or hangover will start to show through to your visitors as the long day wears on. Your staff must wear an identifying badge or symbol. The organiser will probably provide this, and it will not only allow identification and admission but also distinguish salesmen from visitors to the stand, avoiding potential embarrassment.

POSITIONING ON THE STAND

The positions your staff take up will take into account the traffic flow up and down the adjoining gangways. They must not obscure the special displays, and wherever they stand they must look welcoming. They must avoid a guard-like stance which seems to suggest 'Keep off!', and equally a position on the extreme edge of the stand which smacks of the 'Roll up!' tout, a certain deterrent to the visitor at a professional exhibition. But if the stand has been properly designed, the designer, in conjunction with your sales team, will already have determined staff positions.

APPROACHING THE VISITOR

The salesman must not pounce on the visitor, who won't care to be instantly accosted and must have time to get his bearings. Don't hover either, as though waiting for the moment to strike, and never stalk him from behind. But equally, don't avoid him; you must be the one to open the conversation. How you do this is crucial. Never start with 'Can I help you?' or any other question capable of the conversation-stopping answer 'No'. Develop a repertoire of alternative openings: perhaps a comment on what he is looking at, or 'Have you ever used our . . .?', 'Are you involved in specifying?', 'How does this compare with your current equipment?' and the like. You must get him talking to you. Only by doing this can you judge his status, and avoid swamping him with technical jargon or being taken by him into waters too deep for you. Try at the outset to establish his identity, his name, his company and his status. He could be an important buyer making his first approach, a casual drifter, a competitor checking on your products or even someone from head office paying an incognito visit to see how things are going.

RECORDING VISITORS

Once you have placed him, you must make a written record of his identity, not on the back of an envelope but on specially prepared enquiry forms. If you do this you will avoid the disaster of proposing to visit him after the exhibition and failing to turn up. Better not to approach him at all than to allow this to happen. You may need to pass him on then and there to specialist or senior staff; have a goodwill tactic ready in case the person he should meet is occupied for the moment – not necessarily a drink but your house journal or press reports or perhaps a brief discussion about some of your other products.

TYPES OF VISITOR

There are three main groups of visitor: the interested, the fringe visitor who may become a customer, and the distinctly uninterested and largely irrelevant. Beyond these are sub-groups. Among them is the established customer, an old friend. Don't spend too long having agreeable drinks with him; your job is to find new customers and make new sales. Then there is the free-loader. The news must not get about that you run a 'wet' stand; this will be as debilitating to your business as it is to your liver. And the student: remember that he may one day become a very important client, but it is unlikely that the Chairman will want to talk to him there and then. Or the time waster, the monopolising bore: an urgent phone call is a familiar and useful device here, or you may with luck be able to introduce him to a like-minded fellow visitor. Or the complainer: the stand is the last place for dealing with customer complaints. A properly prepared information folder will tell you who at head office is the person to refer him to. Be vigilant for possible spies from competitors, and beware of firms claiming to be doing market research. If a photographer appears, find out what publication he is working for and notify your press officer so that he can follow it up. If you are appearing in the photographs yourself, don't mask any product, or the company name, and never allow loungers, dirty cups or litter to appear in them.

KEEPING STAFF FRESH AND EFFECTIVE

You are going to get very tired from standing about. Get away for regular meal breaks and if at all possible go out of the hall altogether and into the fresh air. But never leave the stand or the hall without telling the stand manager where you are going and for how long. As the exhibition goes on, take care not to let your stand get a lived-in look, with bored or blasé staff doing crossword puzzles or sitting in chairs meant for visitors, with display items left on the floor, or with dirty cups, full ashtrays, thermos flasks, briefcases and carrier bags cluttering the scene and destroying the effect your designer has worked so hard to achieve.

Always have an ample supply of brochures, but don't arrange them in so immaculately geometric a pattern that the visitor may hesitate to disturb it. Don't hand out your most expensive brochures to visiting school parties, or to the familiar I'm-only-here-for-the-pamphlets jackdaws. It may well be more prudent, and more convenient for the visitor, for you to post your more expensive literature to him rather than to hand it out on the spot.

Finally, don't be overwhelmed by the novelty of the situation. Manning a stand can be an experience so theatrical, so convivial, that it may delude staff into thinking that trade exhibitions are mounted to promote the exciting business of exhibiting. They are not. They are mounted to promote trade, and every conversation, every enquiry, and all hospitality, must lead back to a direct sale or the possibility of one, to an appointment to call after the exhibition ends, or, at the very least, to the name and address of a potential customer.

7 The Stand: Before, During and After

GETTING YOUR STAND BUILT

The heart of the matter is getting your stand completed in good time, and this means by press day, not opening day. Normally you will employ a designer, and he will produce the drawings and other information necessary for the contractor to build the stand. You yourself should understand the tendering process even though it is being carried out on your behalf by your designer. He must provide identical information to every contractor, so that each of them may price and quote on exactly the same basis. For a normal exhibition stand in the UK this information will probably comprise drawings, plans, elevations, sections and details of the job, with a written description dealing with the rules and regulations laid down both by the owners of the hall and by the exhibition organisers. This subject is dealt with more fully on pages 60–70.

THE CONTRACTOR

'Horses for courses' must be the rule in selecting the contractor. He must be capable of producing the kind of stand you want, but there is no point in going to a really expensive contractor if your installation is merely a few photographic panels placed inside a shell scheme. Information about contractors can be obtained not only from your designer but also from business and exhibition directories, trade magazines and even the Yellow Pages; and it is worth taking time going to see the work of a few exhibition contractors, especially if you are going to put out a lot of exhibition work during the year.

In this area of contracting work, estimates may vary enormously. There are three main reasons for this. Popular contractors may price high because of overwork and the consequent need to sub-contract. Or a large contractor will have very much higher overheads – but his work will generally be of a higher quality too. Finally, if you leave it late, contractors will already have full order books and will charge a lot more for the late working involved at all levels of their company. Seek as much advice as you can on the subject. In any event, you should ask your designer for a clear indication of probable costs so that you have some picture of what the quotations are likely to be; any good designer will be able to do this.

THE DESIGNER, THE CONTRACTOR AND LABOUR RELATIONS

In both the UK and the USA the contractor's labour force will belong to recognised trade unions, and there will be laid down procedures and agreed time schedules. Do not interfere with these procedures, and never lift a hammer yourself. And however slowly things may seem to be going, do not give the contractor instructions for any alterations on site or change his instructions without consulting the designer. Not only do changes and extras cost a great deal, but the designer is fairly certain to have a clause written into the contract stipulating that he alone is responsible for instructing the contractor. Controlling him must be in the hands of one person only, the person specifically instructed in the tender documents to carry out the job on behalf of the client. All instructions must be in writing so that any extras can be checked against the original brief; and though, in a good professional relationship, informal discussion can usually handle the almost inevitable last minute alterations and additions, these must be followed up by written confirmation.

THE NOMINATED CONTRACTOR: PROS AND CONS

It is sound practice, especially if your company is much involved in exhibition work, to build up a regular working relationship with a particular contractor. But if you have no established contractor you must consider using one of the nominated contractors at a particular show. For international exhibitions in remote countries this may well be good policy, because the nominated contractor will have access to many items which are not available to other contractors. He will also have local expertise and contacts which your usual contractor, visiting the place for the first and perhaps the only time, cannot be expected to have. On the other hand the nominated contractor at any exhibition is usually snowed under with work, particularly if he is responsible for the entire shell scheme, and you are likely to need a good deal of patience.

THE DESIGNER AND THE CONTRACT

The second part of this book has a good deal to say about the whole process of designing, constructing and organising your stand, and the third part provides a number of standard letters and the like for help in carrying through the tendering sequence. But it is usual for this whole aspect of the work to be carried out for you by the designer as part of the service he provides.

RUNNING THE EXHIBIT

We have reached the point where you have a willing and trained staff to look after a completed stand which is ready to open for business. We must now tackle the whole matter of managing and running the stand throughout the exhibition.

PRESS DAY

Press day, usually the day before opening, is the occasion when people from television, film, magazines, trade journals and newspapers come for their preview. As was made clear in the section on the press, you will do all you can to make contact with the media. The organisers' press office arranges the day's programme; find out from them the timing of any official statements and who of consequence is going to be there. Some you may know personally and will want specifically to invite to your stand. If you don't know any media people try to devise a special attraction to persuade them to visit your stand. The traditional lures of 'cheesecake' and abundant liquor are not always the best solution. The press are working to a deadline, they have a great deal to do, and insistent invitations to imbibe alcohol may be an actual disincentive to them. Having something happen on your stand – a demonstration that moves, or a part of your manufacturing process – can do much to attract television cameramen and photographers. But whatever you do, your press release and photographs must be prepared in ample time, and your stand and staff must be ready. The press will not feature an incomplete or unstaffed stand. Your completion day, then, must not be opening day but the eve of press day.

OPENING DAY   Will everything be complete in time for the opening? That last minute flurry may not do the trick, and you should have a plan ready in case. Some of the reasons (though not all of them) why stands are not ready in time are beyond your control, such as strikes, transport holdups, even a thunderstorm. Often these problems will hit everyone in the hall alike, and exhibitors and organisers must co-operate to solve them. And your designer may well have solutions to some of them, either ready to hand or improvised. There may be some way you can turn your predicament to advantage, perhaps by providing a special news story for the press.

If you have some connection with the VIP who is opening the exhibition, have a word with the organiser and try to attach yourself to the official opening tour. But whether or not this is the case, don't lose the useful opportunity which opening day provides to assess the reaction of visitors to your display. In the light of the first day's experience you may find that some slight alteration in the positioning of your staff, or a shift, even if only an inch or two, of one or more exhibits can make a real difference to the way the stand works for the whole of the rest of the exhibition. So you must not look on opening day as a final date after which no modifications can take place.

STAND STAFF   Nor is opening day the only time when your staff need to be really alert and fully functioning. On the contrary, though this is easier to say than to achieve, their performance should improve steadily as the show continues. We have touched already on their relationship with visitors: getting them to stop, to come onto the stand, talking to them, finding who they are, sorting them into significant or irrelevant groups, handling awkward questions. Everyone on the stand must realise the very special nature of this occasion. For most of the year your company is perhaps only seen as an advertisement in the trade press or heard as a voice at the end of the phone. But at the exhibition here it is, in person so to speak, and directly on show. Here is a bunch of real people for customers to see and meet. No matter how efficient your company is, the potential client will take away the wrong impression if either exhibit or staff are sloppy or messy or ill-prepared. Brusque or inattentive staff can destroy the impact of a first-class stand or even the image of a friendly and efficient company to do business with.

The need to record every visitor and every enquiry should again be underlined. Triplicate pads (for head office, sales office and exhibition files) are often obtainable from the organisers. Start following up enquiries right away; don't let them pile up until after the exhibition ends. Apart from any other consideration, if the exhibition runs for three or four weeks, a first-day enquirer who has no communication from you for a month is likely by then to have bought what he wants from a competitor.

STAND MAINTENANCE

Like any other working space your stand is going to get dirty. It needs careful cleaning and maintenance and the making good of any damage. If you have proper cleaning and housekeeping materials it is possible to maintain a stand which by the close of the exhibition does not look as though everyone has been living in it for the last month. But you will not achieve this unless you plan for it and unless your staff realise how imperative it is.

The structure itself must keep its brightness, and may need more than just regular cleaning and dusting. Night sheets are sometimes provided to cover the stand during closing hours and these keep out a modicum of dirt and mess. But a large number of people inevitably brings with it wear and tear and you may need a maintenance agreement with your contractor for him to come in after hours and carry out any necessary repainting or refurbishment. In any event, check whether he is going to another city or another country when he finishes your stand. Anything really badly damaged which can't be repaired on site is better removed if at all possible rather than left broken for all to see.

Keep a log of all faults, repairs and changes carried out, for it is unusual to have a specific repairs clause in your contract, and your contractor will charge you for any emergency repairs or other activity you ask him to do during the run of the exhibition. When the exhibition ends the log should not be despatched to your vaults, but held for the Exhibit Manager of your next show. Otherwise he does not get the benefit of last time's experience, starts again with a blank slate, and probably makes some of the same mistakes all over again.

HOSPITALITY AND REFRESHMENTS

Throughout the exhibition you will want to offer refreshment of some sort to your visitors. Do you provide alcohol? Many exhibitors do, and thereby contribute to the popular fallacy that modern exhibitions are gin palaces. There is a good deal to be said for not joining them.

Your visitors can't be left to drink alone, and nothing wears your staff down faster than repeatedly downing large gins with a succession of visitors. Nor is there anything worse than intoxicated or hungover staff. Drunks cause problems everywhere, not least in exhibition halls, and the organisers will not thank you for pouring out alcohol too liberally. You are there to dispense product information and sales talk, not liquor; and fruit juice, minerals, tea and coffee are generally far more appropriate. This way you avoid being stuck with free-loaders, but if this does happen to you your staff must know the system for getting them to move on. The situation will need polite and discreet handling if, as occasionally happens, someone from a major client turns out to be a free-loader. But of course they don't put in a great deal of time on dry stands. Lastly, remember that the process of eating and drinking is a messy one. Keep the preparation area for food and drink out of sight, and clear away the debris quickly. Be houseproud of your exhibit.

TRADE LITERATURE We have already spoken of the need to control the distribution of your brochures, leaflets and other giveaways, especially the more expensive ones. It may be better to take the names and addresses of enquirers who want the latter, and post them on later (but not much later). A cheap and simple information sheet is useful for universal distribution; and you will be surprised at how quickly they run out unless you take care to have and maintain an ample supply. A daily logging system should give you a suitable means of controlling day-to-day stocks not only of trade literature but also of drinks and refreshments.

AFTER THE EXHIBITION ### Paying for services and supplies
You will need a number of services during the exhibition, from security surveillance to cleaning, fresh flowers and a hundred and one other small housekeeping items. You must order these, follow the order with written instructions, and agree how you are to pay for them. Overseas, as we have pointed out, this is a serious problem. It will be to your advantage to pay cash on supply (if you can obtain it) because the bills for all services incurred may have to be cleared before you are allowed to leave the exhibition hall. Cheques may not be acceptable (and remember that bank cards often cover you only up to a limit of £50 sterling). Travellers' cheques may help, as also of course will ready cash, provided you take care not to be robbed. Best of all is a cashing arrangement with a local bank.

But whatever method you use it is imperative that you get a written receipt to the effect that payment in full has been made. Otherwise a bill may reach you months later for services already paid for. All this may sound elementary, but if it is not done systematically you may find yourself in real difficulties as you dash to the airport after an overseas exhibition.

Follow-up publicity
Many exhibitors rush away after the show and forget all about it in their worry about the next one on the list or their pleasure to be getting home. But the exhibition itself is only the beginning of increased business for your company.

To realise the full potential of an expensive show you should put out a press release when it ends. A very good way of underlining your presence at the exhibition is to get suitable stories, of a major contract signed or some other special achievement or event, into the post-show issues of the trade press. Just as you must follow up – and fast – all client enquiries received during the exhibition, so you must follow up the press. Of course it is much harder to get reviews into post-show articles than into previews in the same magazine because there will not be nearly as much advertising support when the exhibition is over, but with a good story given to the right person it is far from impossible, and well worth trying, especially if you are yourself a regular advertiser in the magazine in question. You organised your preview publicity. Equally, you must organise your follow-up.

Evaluation

How do you learn the lessons of the exhibition, and record them against the next show you intend to participate in? It is useful to start logging these lessons while the exhibition is still in progress, when it is all fresh in your mind. Talk, too, to the organisers after the event. Have they provided services which turned out not to be of any great use to you, or not provided services you would have welcomed? By the end of the show you should be on excellent terms with them, and they will appreciate your comments, which may help them to stage a better show next time.

An overall guard book – keep a guard book which gathers together all information, from locations and stand drawings to forms and notes on the effectiveness of particular details. And don't bury it after the show; it will be invaluable for the exhibit manager next time. In the case of an overseas exhibition, get a copy of the guard book to your local agent.

Attendances – produce notes, too, of attendance figures, including a set of the organisers' daily news. Some organisers research into numbers and types of visitors; these audits should be filed for your future use. A little time devoted to collating this kind of information will be immensely helpful to you in deciding whether, in the event, it was worth your participating in this particular exhibition.

Re-use of your display – can any part of your exhibit be re-used? It may be that parts can be used again in showrooms or reception areas or even in the factory canteen, where the costs can be spread over other budgets. But even if that nicely designed display wall at the back of the stand was expensive, it will probably be uneconomic to store it against next year's exhibition. By the time it has been taken down, shipped and stored you will almost certainly have spent more than it would cost you to rebuild it from scratch next time, though specially made exhibit supports and similar items may be worth storing.

A post-exhibition conference – if you have the chance, organise a post-mortem on the whole enterprise, bringing together everyone who had any part to play, the entire exhibit team, the designer and possibly the contractor as well. It is not only you and your stand staff who will have useful things to say. Your designer will almost certainly contribute comments which will make the next stand even better. And remember that you can learn not only from your own display but also from those of your competitors as well. They may have found better solutions than your team did to particular aspects, and there is nothing at all to stop you using and developing their ideas next time.

PLANNING THE KEY TO SUCCESS

Over the years, if you follow these routines, you cannot fail to become better at the whole business of exhibiting. But the really important lesson remains: think ahead, organise, make certain everyone knows what is expected of him from start to finish, and keep to all timetables and deadlines.

In practical terms you will find that it is far more sensible to programme a consecutive series of deadlines for successive stages rather than simply driving straight towards that single final deadline of the hour before the arrival of the press in the hall. A deadline for the designer's preliminary design, a deadline for briefing your stand staff, and so on through the whole process: this series of individual deadlines will make overall control much simpler. You will get the job progressively and systematically done instead of ending up in that familiar, impossible situation of trying to get five hundred tiny details completed in the last half hour. Organise your planning really well and you may even be able to sit back and watch the panic among fellow exhibitors. This is a highly desirable position to achieve, for without disciplined organisation many exhibitors are so exhausted by opening day that their clients find them with bags under their eyes, icepacks on their heads and sleep in their minds.

Make certain this never happens to you.

1 *Empty hall*

4 *Wednesday 20th*

2 *Monday 18th*

5 *Thursday 21st*

6 *Friday 22nd*

3 *Tuesday 19th*

7 *Saturday 23rd*

8 *Open period 24th–30th*

10 *Monday 2nd*
11 *Wednesday 4th*

9 *Sunday 1st*

CONSTRUCTION: OPEN AND BREAKDOWN PERIODS

Exhibits don't stand on their own at an exhibition. Plans, models and preparatory drawings often show the stand without surrounding clutter and confusing messages. However, not only does the stand when working have to act and work in relation to other surrounding exhibits, it has to compete against the crowds of people moving on and around the stand itself.

The stand has to be so designed that it can be built up from within its own confines, as you can't rely upon space in the surrounding gangways being available. You might have six working days to construct a complicated stand but you will seldom have more than two days to demolish it. This timed photograph was taken every day during the build-up and breakdown of The Building Exhibition in Birmingham, England.

Other industries have shorter build-up periods, so it is essential to examine the design of the stand and determine how long you need to construct your exhibit and how much can be prefabricated by your contractor.

Remember: you take over clean space at the beginning of your tenancy and it must be left equally clean at the end.

Part Two
DESIGNING YOUR EXHIBIT

8 The Design Process

This section of the book makes no claim to provide any perfect solutions to the problems of trade exhibit design. At the heart of success is the vital ingredient of creativity, and this cannot be captured within the covers of a book. Our aim is simply to supply a map of the route to success, calling attention to obstacles and pitfalls along the way and establishing a systematic course to follow.

ORGANISING THE DESIGN PROCESS

The process involves many people. Firstly there is the client himself, represented by the chief executive, and the exhibit manager. Then there is the exhibition organiser, responsible for the whole show; there is the exhibition hall or venue owner, the person who owns the place where the exhibition is being mounted; there is the contractor, whose skills lie in the specialist field of exhibition construction; there is the designer, who produces the design you want and supervises its construction and production; and there is your own advertising agency and marketing department, which must ensure that all exhibition work is geared to, and advances, your overall marketing policy. All these parties are interdependent, but the most important relationship is that between designer and client, who must understand each other, get on well together and be able to work as a single central directing team.

CHOOSING YOUR DESIGNER

The designer creates and realises the design and production of your stand, supervises the integration of the various specialists and sub-contractors, and in effect acts throughout as your agent. He and his work must be suitable for the kind of stand you need. But you will choose him not only on the

evidence of work he has already done but also on the basis of how he will get on with you and your company, whether you like him and could work well with him.

The kinds of designer available to you have already been discussed on pp. 29–31. To summarise: your likeliest choice is a freelance designer, but remember that he may not always find it easy to come to terms with your needs since he will not know your business as well as someone who actually works for you. However, your in-house designer may have become rather stale in design terms just because he is always working with your products, and he may also lack experience of full-scale exhibition work, which is very different from the design of publicity leaflets. It is vital that you use someone experienced in exhibition and design work. This could point towards the exhibition contractor's design team, but they too may have difficulties in that their employer may require them to use systems or pieces of structure left over from previous exhibitions in order economically to utilise existing stock. Indeed you may find that the contractor's team are prejudiced in favour of large structures simply because they earn more money, though they may be quite unnecessary or unsuitable for the kind of exhibit you require.

THE BRIEF

Whether you choose an independent designer, an in-house designer or a designer from the contractor's organisation, all will follow the same basic sequence in carrying out the work for you.

The design sequence has three main stages, but before Stage One can begin you must write the brief. Clients have been known to panic over this and to produce something wholly inadequate. For the purposes of this book we assume that you are using an independent designer since he is the person

It is a good idea when attending an exhibition and taking photographs to start with your own badge. This gives the name of the exhibition, the name of the photographer and also the date and is a very useful way of remembering vital information later on.

who will need most information from you, particularly if he has not worked for your company before.

The brief will naturally vary widely according to the nature and scale of the exhibition. But the designer will always need full information about your company, its marketing policy and why it is in business; about the products to be shown; about the hall, the particular site and any constraints these impose; about the way you intend the display to work; and about staffing and housekeeping. The following checklist should enable you to compile a brief which does not omit anything crucial. Individual elements in it are discussed at length elsewhere in the book.

1 *Company information*
   Aims
   Marketing policy
   Position in the market place; and competitors
   Reasons for participation
   Proposed message
(Note: briefing should include visits by designer to your factory, works, office)

2 *Products to be displayed*
   Number; size; weight
   Special shelving; assembly

3 *Constraints*
   Rules and regulations of hall owners
   Rules and regulations of exhibition organisers
   Safety regulations and fire risks

4 *Site*
   Overall plan of hall
   Physical features of site, with any limitations
   Location of aisles
   Likely flow pattern of visitors

5 *Layout and housekeeping*
   Staff: number present at any one time
       : their positioning
       : the nature of their duties
       : number of sales points
   Literature display facilities
   Phone, telex, computer, audio-visual facilities
   Office accommodation
   Refreshment arrangements
   Stores: for literature stocks
       : for refreshments
       : for coats etc. (visitors' and staff's)
       : for cleaning material

6 *Design requirements*
   Perspectives, elevations, working drawings etc.
   Model

7 *Construction, maintenance and removal*
   Responsibility for: construction supervision
                   : instruction of contractor
                   : written instructions for all
                     extras
                   : integration of all specialist
                     and sub-contracting work
                   : ensuring maintenance
                     throughout exhibition
                   : timetabling of entire
                     operation
                   : ensuring adherence to
                     timetable
                   : return of exhibits and
                     removal of stand equipment

THE DESIGN SEQUENCE: STAGE ONE

Having satisfied yourself that the brief is agreed by the key departments of your company, and that your chosen designer can best achieve this brief, you should now proceed with the initial contract letter.

The contract letter
The initial part of this first stage is the drawing up by the designer of a fee letter or contract document. This sets out details of what he understands by the brief which has been given to him, the fees and likely

During the build-up period in an exhibition hall, no signs are visible. Signs usually go up at the last minute and it is not until all the competition is up and around that you can see how your own design stands out from the crowd.

expenses for providing his services, a basic outline work programme and a paragraph asking for a formal contract to be provided. Part Three of this book contains a typical outline letter.

The design proposals

Unless the brief is inadequate or the project unusually complicated, it will not take the designer very long to research it and assimilate the information he has been given. He may need to visit people in your company to find out more about the purposes of the product and your system for its design, manufacture and marketing. But he will soon come back to you with an outline design proposal.

The outline of the design may be in words, but will be accompanied by drawings or other visuals. However splendid these are, you must ask him to provide also a simple cardboard scale model so that you can see the proposed design in three dimensions, and use it for planning how the stand staff will

work in practice and for briefing both the exhibition contractors and your own staff. A cardboard model will save you and your staff a great deal of time, help to avoid misunderstanding and add enormously to the final success of your participation. Most people cannot easily understand plans or perspective drawings, and a simple model will help them check out their requirements before arriving on opening day – and starting to demand changes!

Fees and expenses: Stage One

At this point Stage One is completed and the designer will invoice you for fees and expenses to date. This may be on the basis of a percentage fee agreed on estimated overall costs, or simply on an hourly rate. Or it may be on a fixed basis, where an exact fee for the whole job has been agreed at the outset and the first one-third is due at the end of the first stage. At the same time all expenses (travel costs, telex and long-distance phone calls, cost of prints and dyelines, and incidental out-of-pocket expenses) will be charged, usually at actual cost, or (by prior arrangement) including also a small percentage handling fee.

An eye-catching object can be very helpful, especially if it attracts other people from surrounding areas to see what it is. It can usually be enhanced with signs, words or logos.

STAGE TWO

Stage Two begins once the client agrees that the designer's proposals are satisfactory and that everything is now set to go forward. In essence this stage consists of turning the outline design into the actuality of the real thing. The main task for the designer is to produce the tender documents, including working drawings, specifications and all the other information the contractor needs to build the stand, together with the necessary permissions to carry out the work, such as fire and safety approvals.

Tendering

The designer goes out to a number of contractors with identical information, asking each to quote a price. Quotation normally takes between a fortnight and a month, depending on the job's complexity, and designer and client then jointly decide which contractor to use. A typical letter inviting tenders and a checklist of items covered by the specification will be found in Part Three. We have already said that 'horses for courses' is the rule in choosing contractors. For very simple jobs, such as putting photographic panels into a shell scheme, specially written tender documents are not really necessary; tendering notes to go with the outline drawings and artwork are enough.

Tenders high and low

Some tenders may be surprisingly high, because the contractor has more work than he can handle and needs to sub-contract, or because a late invitation to tender will involve him in overtime payments. Some contractors have an irritating habit, too, of tendering absurdly high (rather than simply saying that they are too busy to take the job on) in order to keep their names on your books. Conversely, an absurdly low tender should be ignored. Either the

Trucks and machines are exciting objects in their own right. Nevertheless they may need special signs for exhibition purposes.

contractors' work. Again, you yourself may want to use a particular person for a particular special job, such as painting your mural or doing the interior design work. If so, the designer must make clear in the tender documents that he is nominating this person for the job, and he will write in suitable clauses to ensure that the contractor grants him all necessary access and support. As with any building site the contractor is responsible for safety and access, and without prior arrangement he will not allow anyone other than his own staff to work on the site. If sub-contracting part of the work becomes necessary, make sure that the lines of responsibility and reporting are clearly understood. Much aggravation will be avoided and the risks of overspending will be reduced.

contractor has not estimated correctly or he is desperate for work. In the latter case, and if you are particularly unlucky, he may be out to squeeze as much as he possibly can from you and your designer, and throughout the job a battle of wills will rage between you and the contractor, who may even go bankrupt after you have paid for the stand but before you have taken delivery. Your designer's experience will be invaluable in indicating to you the broad level at which the quotations should lie.

Sub-contracting

Most British contractors work mainly in the timber and painting side of exhibitions and rarely have metalworking, photographic, plastic or other material workshops within their organisation, preferring to subcontract this area. If so, stipulate that they are responsible to you for their sub-

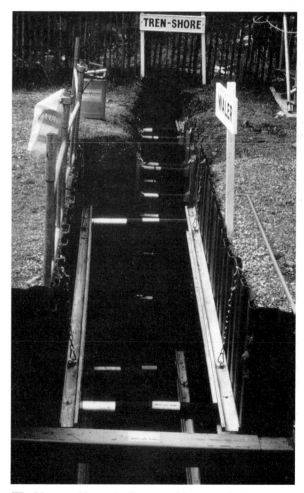

Working machinery is always exciting, especially if the rubbish and offcuts can be kept out of view of visitors.

A packing case, specially designed to go into the hold of an aircraft, tells a great deal about the export-mindedness of exhibitors.

It is very difficult to design an island site that is interesting from all four sides. A back wall can be extremely helpful but you should always give a certain amount of information for the casual visitor, to make sure that he continues around the corner to see what is behind.

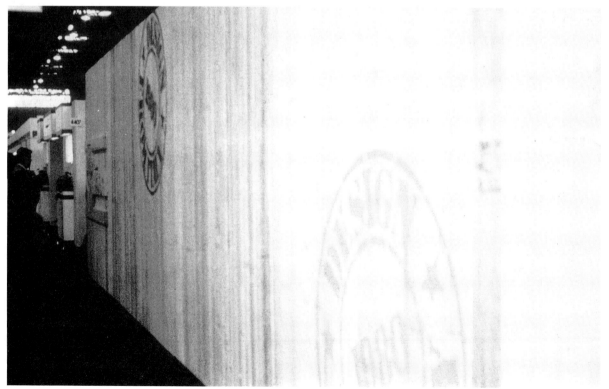

Free-standing design areas with different information for different users of the same product are a good way of using large spaces. The use of a free-standing box to anchor corners of the stand and to identify the stand number provides good orientation for visitors.

When designing rows of stands facing each other down a gangway, it is essential for the nameboard to be at right angles to the stand so that visitors approaching from either direction can see the name of the company ahead of them. Don't forget that if this is on a wall divider there will be a different name on the other side.

The workforce

Unless your specialist is a member of the appropriate union you will be in trouble if the venue is a commercial hall such as Olympia, Earls Court, the National Exhibition Centre, Madison Square Gardens or the Dallas Superbowl. The union situation is much less difficult than it used to be, but you must still make sure that a specialist working on site is a union member. Some features, of course, can be produced off site and delivered as a completed unit so that union members in your contractor's firm can install it.

There are also working rule agreements with the unions in the United Kingdom which specify very precisely the amounts and duration of time that various trades can work in the major exhibition halls. Many exhibitions are put in during the weekend, but gone are the days when you could pay extra to the workforce and expect them to work through the night so as to finish by press day.

An example of a stand which was probably designed to be seen from the other side of the gangway. The dividing walls carry no identification or indication as to what is on show, so the exhibitor on the other side of the gangway is likely to benefit from the attention.

Fire extinguishers cause obstructions and should always be placed on the stand. If the name of the company appears on the fascia and not at right angles to the stand it becomes difficult to see in advance whom you are approaching.

Nowadays there are strict regulations about such things as weekend working. But never under-estimate the workforce – and never knock in that last nail yourself when the panic is on. The things the workforce can achieve in the last few hours have to be seen to be believed; so don't interfere, and don't ever take matters into your own hands. Remember the pride most people take in their work, and their wish and ability to finish and produce a good job in time.

Hire services

You should realise that most exhibition contractors provide a hire service for standard floors and wall panels in the United Kingdom, and for drapes, poles, carpeting and the like in the United States. The larger firms will also have on hire a series of modular exhibition systems which will allow you to build anything from a few panels on supports to a complete shell scheme. You will need your designer's advice here. It is normal procedure in

Chairs are always welcome and will attract visitors, but the more comfortable they are the longer the visitor is likely to stay. It very often happens that those most in need of the seats have the least need for the information. It is always a waste to have a side wall with a photograph but without a clear caption.

Britain and to some degree in the United States to hire the complete structure from the contractor. If so, all of it, including your specially designed features, will be taken away at the end. None of it automatically becomes your property unless you have clearly established with the contractor that you are buying your specially designed feature and not merely hiring it. Reputable contractors will not put you into difficulties in this situation, but even so they will consider that everything is on hire unless you explicitly establish otherwise from the outset. The cost of buying or hiring a feature is often very much the same, but if you want to re-use it, then there will be additional charges for packing, transport, storage and refurbishing at a later date.

Alterations and extras

In the contract documents will be a clause stating that the designer alone is responsible for instructing the contractor. This is not because he wants to prevent your involvement with your own stand but because without a single clear channel of authority you are likely to end up with an invoice from the contractor containing one major statement of the overall cost and 25 pages of extras charged for but not quoted for, covering odd tasks you asked him to do in the panic of the moment. If, for instance, you ask him to put in an extra light fitting to illuminate a part of the stand which seems unduly dark, this may well end by costing you more than the total existing light contract. You will be charged not only for the fitting but also perhaps for sending a lorry at an hour's notice to collect it from the electrical supplier. Then there is the connection charge, the recabling, and if the worst comes to the worst and the new unit results in overloading, the cost of arranging for more electricity from the main hall supply.

Spur-of-the-moment decisions made in an effort to get things done in a hurry are always expensive. Nor should they be necessary. If your designer has done his job properly he will have allowed, should he have any doubt about the number of lights required, a sum in the contract to cover possible extra lamps and lighting; and he will also have instructed the contractor to allow for enough power in the wiring of the stand should that extra lamp really be needed.

The designer, then, must be responsibile for controlling the contractor. If he does need to add any extras he will always give instructions in writing

so that when the invoice comes in he can check those extras against the instructions issued at the time. Ideally he should seek quotations for them, but the right contractor can be trusted to give you a pretty good idea of likely costs by word of mouth. Nevertheless the instructions must be confirmed in writing so that everyone knows where he is when it comes to sending in and clearing the invoices.

Alterations will also cost a good deal. If you decide to wrap that plywood panel in red felt rather than the green originally specified, your contractor has probably by now already bought the green felt and will be quite within his rights to charge you for both. If you have to issue additional instructions or alterations, do it as early as possible; the later you do it, the more it is likely to cost.

When it is certain, or almost certain, that there will be additional things needed but their exact cost is not yet known, your designer can put in 'pc' or 'ps' sums. 'pc' stands for prime cost, and he uses this when he knows exactly how much the item will cost. For instance, if you want a particular chair on your stand which costs £35, you will ask the contractor, through your designer, to include a pc sum of £35 for the chair in his tender. If you then change your mind and want a more expensive chair, he will charge you the extra over £35; if you choose one that costs less he will still charge you the pc sum of £35. If the designer does a 'ps' sum, i.e. a preliminary sum, you can assume that the contractor will charge only the actual cost of the item, whether it is more or less than the sum allowed.

All these procedures are of course much easier if you have built up a regular relationship with a particular contractor, and it often pays to spend slightly more on using a really good contractor to whom you can confidently leave a good deal of the detailed work.

Fees and expenses: Stage Two

Stage Two is completed immediately before the start of build-up on site. Your designer will have prepared his second invoice together with a statement of expenses incurred to date, and this is the time for him to submit it. Remember that independent designers with small offices are never over-capitalised, and even if you have already made an advance against expenses his bill should be paid by return.

A high wall with the minimum of information means that everybody looks in the opposite direction. Large numbers of visitors using this gangway in either direction will fail to notice the participation of the firm, even though it has taken a very large space.

STAGE THREE

Supervision

The actual production and erection of the stand take place during Stage Three. We have already underlined how essential it is that the control of the job is left to the designer; one of the surest ways of letting a job go out of control is for everyone, however remotely involved, to start giving oral instructions to the contractor. If the client himself wants a change made he must get it done through his designer so that at every point throughout the process one person has control and is responsible for knowing the current position on what is being done and its effect on costs.

Since the designer has been in charge all along, there should be no real problems when the final invoices come in after the project is finished. The designer is responsible for collating and checking these invoices, and the results are very likely to fall well into line with what the client is expecting.

Contractor's liability

On the completion of the stand the designer is also responsible for the process of accepting the work carried out by the contractor. If it is a permanent installation there may well be a liability period within which, should any substandard work start to show its failings, the designer is entitled to call the contractor back to repair and make good the work at his own expense, to the standard originally stipulated. Even if it is a stand at a short-term exhibition, make sure that your designer knows the whereabouts of your contractor in case of a catastrophe or even of a need for some simple maintenance. Your contractor and all his staff may already have moved to another town, and maintenance cannot wait.

Wrapping up the project

Details of the type of clauses to be included in the original specification to cover these various aspects

A very good example of a well-known international logo clearly displayed and giving a strong identification to the stand.

will be found in Part Three. On completion of the work the designer will return to the client any photographs and other original material which he has borrowed to produce the stand design, along with all other file information, including the official guide to the exhibition, which will be useful next time round.

Fees and expenses: Stage Three

At the end of Stage Three the designer will send you his third, and normally final, design fees and expenses invoices. If the project has been carried out on the basis of the actual cost of the job with the fee as a percentage of that, the third fee invoice will be the one which finally adjusts the fee to actual costs incurred. If the job has involved a permanent installation, 10% or 15% of the fees may be held back just as the contractor's fees, probably to the same percentage, are held back. The balance becomes due on the final approvals at the end of the liability period in six or twelve months' time. Every project varies in its requirements. A small window display needs little of the detail described here; a very large international exhibition may need a lot more besides.

Part Three contains a number of specimen documents which will help the client or designer to understand the process of tendering and supervising the project, whether it be large or small.

9 Communication and Circulation

WHO ARE YOUR VISITORS?

The design of your stand will be fundamentally affected by who your target visitors are. Is the exhibition a trade show restricted to a particular trade or industry? Or is it a public exhibition, open to anyone who pays to come in? Either way, you must decide very early on what kind of visitor you are aiming at. If you do not attract the right visitor, if he does not have the right reaction to your exhibit, if he does not go away with the right message, then you have wasted your time, money and effort.

WHY ARE YOU EXHIBITING?

You must decide what you hope to achieve by showing at a particular exhibition. Incidentally, if you find it hard to put together a convincing list of aims, then you may well do better not to participate at all. This may sound obvious, but a surprising number of companies exhibit almost automatically year after year at certain exhibitions without ever really considering why they are there. Very often the money they spend on lavish stands could be much better used in advertising and in direct postal communication with their clients.

Your marketing strategy will almost certainly call for communication with members of your own industry. For instance, if you are selling drain water pipes, your targets will be builders' merchants, builders, perhaps the farming community and so on; you won't be especially interested in attracting the attention of hairdressers or computer experts.

But you can do a great deal to communicate with those whom you want to contact by the way you circulate information, both in the press and, amongst individual clients, by inviting them to visit your stand. You may be surprised at the number of people who will turn up if you send them a specific invitation to come and see you at 'Stand 89'. Free

tickets, which most organisers will let you have for distribution, are useful here too.

TYPES OF VISITOR

Among your visitors will be those who are simply wandering through the exhibition. They may not have heard of your company at all and have come across you just by chance when walking round a corner. They may already be using one of your competitors, and you will need a boldly inviting display and good salesmanship to attract them to your stand.

Then there is the visitor who always makes a point of coming to your stand, if only to renew friendships and meet your sales staff. Perhaps one of your best customers, he is more interested in maintaining human contacts than in looking at displays of products he may know as well as you do. He is a prime target for any new products you may have and you must make sure he sees them. You must not spend too much time with existing clients, however. They are important, but they are not new business.

The VIP visitor who comes round on opening day is likely to be wholly uninterested in your products. You will therefore need some specially attractive aspect of your display to bring him to your particular stand. Why do you need a visit from him? The answer of course is the press and publicity people, especially the photographers, who follow in his wake. You may well end up with some of the best free publicity imaginable, not just from the exhibition but in your whole publicity campaign.

Trainees and students form another significant group. They will be your future clients, and your staff should spend some time (but not too much) explaining your product and discussing problems with them. The immediate benefit may be hard to see, but in five years' time the exercise may bring you a major contract. Incidentally, you may not

A classic photograph of a carefully planned stand – which closes for lunch each day. How many visitors and potential customers don't take lunch when visiting exhibitions? Always make sure your stand can stay open all day, by organising proper shift working.

The exhibitor should never be comfortably seated and reading something. He will miss a lot of eye contact, some of which may be vital.

want to give them your expensive glossy brochures and you should plan your literature so that there are suitable publications for giving to students and casual visitors.

Lastly there is the unwanted visitor, whose interest is confined to free-loading, either drink or leaflets and other material. We have already explained that these people must be handled with courtesy and discretion. Very often your designer's skills will be useful in achieving a layout which helps your staff to do this.

Exhibitions are very tiring for the visitor, who may have walked several miles by the time he reaches your stand, and you must anticipate his likely state of exhaustion, both mental and physical. He will be dehydrated from the overheating of the hall, hobbling because he was stupid enough not to wear comfortable shoes and generally hot and uncomfortable because he didn't dress for what is quite a physically demanding exercise. And if he has not prepared a list of stands in advance, he will have walked needless miles up and down the aisles, either hunting for you or just wandering aimlessly. So why, in this state, should he bother to come to your stand, and how are you going to provide an environment which will make him want to meet you?

In view of all the competing stands this may seem

impossible, but it is really quite simple. Just get the basics right. Do you have seats on your stand where he can sit (but not so deep and plush that he cannot easily move on)? Do you have a fan circulating air? Is your presentation interesting enough in itself to make him actually want to come and see what you are talking about? All these things are for your designer to consider in the process of designing the stand. If he keeps it simple and plans it all according to the exact requirements you have identified in writing the design brief, you will not go far wrong.

WHAT IS YOUR MESSAGE?

Once you have identified your target audience, the next step is to determine exactly what it is you want

It is very hard to look welcoming when your feet hurt and you are on your own.

Don't let your sales director take a seat and nod off on your stand.

to tell them and how you are going to do it. Establishing the content is of course the first essential; but its presentation must be right too. A golden rule is to use as few words as possible, and these must be easily and quickly understood. This is particularly true in any industry with a complicated vocabulary of its own, as a look round any computer show will bear out. The number of stands with walls covered in gobbledygook, unintelligible to the average visitor, is legion. There is no point in inscribing the words 'dot matrix printer facility' when an illustration at once intelligible to everyone passing the stand will do the trick for you.

What are your competitors doing? If they are telling the same story as you, then it is up to you to find a subtly different approach or twist so that the visitor will distinguish your stand from the others.

Remember that however splendid the message the visitor approaches the stand only gradually and in sequence. The first thing he must see, and from some distance, is an identifying sign. This is why the larger purpose-built stands have a huge company logo riding across the top and visible right over the hall, and why shell stands have a fascia at the highest level to carry the company's name and stand number. Then, as he gets nearer, the basic marketing message should be plainly visible from down the gangway so that he gets it even if he doesn't come onto the stand itself. And so down the line until, once on the stand, he is presented with the detailed information you need to get across to him, both by display techniques of every kind and by personal contact with your staff.

If you want to attract attention, there are many ways of doing it besides using signs and captions.

VISITOR RESPONSE

But how do you get the visitor onto the stand itself, particularly if the stands are set on a 4 inch (100mm) high platform? He has to cross this physical barrier. We have already looked at ways in which the staffing of the stand helps (or hinders) this process, but the design of the stand also can greatly help to attract the visitor. If your site is between two gangways, for instance, the stand should be organised so as implicitly to invite people to use it as a quick cut-through from one gangway to the other. Perhaps you can use some of the techniques employed in retail shop design where the fronts are almost like funnels to suck you in. Or you may have no 'shop front' at all but a stand which comes out imperceptibly to meet the visitor so that he finds he

has wandered in to it without realising it. These matters are an important part of the design process. If you don't give them full weight, visitors will not come, and however well designed your stand is in itself there will then be little point in your exhibiting at all. The illustrations show some examples of the different ways in which you can create visitor response and interest.

VISITOR INVOLVEMENT

So far we have talked mainly about the power of 'stories' – flat graphics – to get visitors to your stand. But never forget the lure of 'happenings'. Engage your visitors' curiosity by involving them, getting them to participate in your exhibit. It may be that you can stage a quiz, or mount some kind of

Somewhere behind this stand there is someone waiting to demonstrate what you can't see until you get really close.

Two members of the staff waiting for the visiting photographer.

demonstration. Or you can give them buttons to push, handles to turn to set things in motion, devices rarely used in trade shows though commonplace in permanent displays and exhibitions. They need not be expensive; indeed, if they were, museums would be most unlikely to use them.

A REST AREA?

Another way of increasing the appeal of your stand is to offer a modest haven or oasis. Visitors are likely to be suffering from blunted minds and sore feet. They will welcome an old-fashioned sit-down if you give them the chance. In the past exhibitors have sometimes won themselves good publicity simply by providing rest areas within the turmoil of the exhibition – so long as it is unmistakably clear to the visitors who is responsible for this oasis. But it has to be well organised and maintained throughout the

exhibition if it is not to end up a pigsty of waste paper and sandwich wrappings.

TAILORING YOUR STAND TO YOUR VISITORS

The kind of visitor you are after will naturally affect the way the stand is designed. If, for example, you are hoping to take orders on the stand, your designer and you may set aside an area with some privacy, a small office perhaps, where contract details can be worked out on the spot, away from the hurly-burly. But bear in mind that exhibition space is not cheap. If you need any substantial area for your stand office it is worth thinking of having a two-level stand with offices above and display below.

Or you may be using the occasion not so much to take sales orders as to get out information about your product, or perhaps simply to show your presence and remind people of how they can get in touch with you. If so, most of the stand will naturally be given over to the public area and

It is a good idea to bring your office onto the stand as long as you are out of sight of the casual visitor.

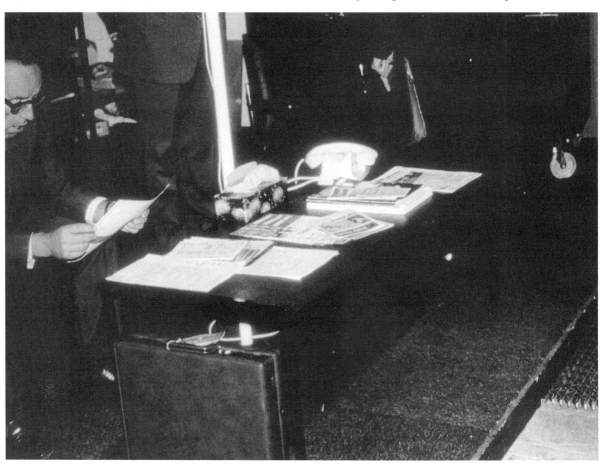

beyond this you will need only a small area for the staff to keep their belongings in and for storing literature and cleaning equipment.

OVERCOMING CIRCULATION PROBLEMS

It may be that you have come to the exhibition late and so have been unable to choose the site you would like. You may end up in what seems an almost impossible position where you think no one will find you at all, perhaps in a remote area under the overhang of the hall's upper level. But a skilful designer can often turn this to advantage, and the organisers too can help you to make the most of it. If they know you have a difficult site they may allow you to disregard the overall rule forbidding signs above your stand or over a prescribed height and size. Even if they don't allow this it is always worth asking, so do make sure your designer talks to the organisers. They have seen many different solutions to problems of this kind and often have considerable design experience themselves. And it is always possible that since you booked, someone else has unexpectedly dropped out of the exhibition and you can move to their site.

THE FIVE SENSES

Your visitors can hear, touch, smell and taste as well as see. So they are more likely to be attracted to an exhibit that moves than to a wholly static display. Fountains and water gardens too can be excellent features. They are most welcome in a hectic setting, and a fountain with seats by it, and a suitable view of the message you want to project, may be very attractive not only to the visitors who are coming your way in any case but also to passers-by who otherwise might not have come. There are many other ways of appealing to the different senses; never forget that your visitor has more than just a pair of eyes and a pair of feet.

PATTERNS OF MOVEMENT

It is a matter of ordinary observation that people often do not move in the way planners believe or want them to. Sometimes, sheeplike, they may dutifully follow the crowd. At other times they will decline to take the direction signalled and ignore all indications that they are expected to go from left to right. And like other animals they will keep to the safety of the edges when they are confronted by large open spaces, rather than striking boldly into the middle. National traits are important too; in the Far East, particularly in Japan, visitors nearly always go through in a group, whereas in Europe and America they tend to strike out on their own. Variations are considerable and in designing for good circulation your designer needs to understand local traits. Italians, for instance, are used to promenading – no fear of big open spaces for them – whilst Americans are reluctant to do any walking at all and will be exhausted by the time their aching feet get them to your stand.

THE LAYOUT OF THE STAND

The way the interior of your stand is to be laid out will be determined by the answer to one overriding question. How do you and your sales staff intend to use it? Will they be selling direct, cementing orders and carrying out business transactions? If so (as we have already pointed out) they will need small office spaces together with refreshment facilities. Sweet tea is as essential in the Middle East as coffee is in the United States.

Or are they giving out information on a revolutionary new product? In that case the product will be the focal point of the whole display, with plenty of space round it so that it can be properly seen, and plenty of storage for the supporting literature they will be distributing. If you are demonstrating the unique capabilities of a new machine, consider having several identical ones on the stand, each with separate staff and support space. This will both increase the number of visitors you can handle at the same time and avoid undue crowding round any one machine; and it will give the intending visitor some freedom of choice over which display he wants to examine, especially if you use different sizes of the same product.

Perhaps the stand will be hardly manned at all, largely running itself. In this case it must be designed accordingly, with information literature clearly available and the main storyline plainly set out, perhaps sequentially, with a single manned contact and information desk at the end of the sequence. But remember that people come at you from at least two directions in most exhibitions.

Are you intending to show a short film at regular intervals? Then you will need a small presentation area, and you must not forget to have the basic information handy for those who arrive when the presentation is halfway through or just finished; they may not wait for the next showing.

All these variants and many more will affect your designer's planning and enable him to produce an interior design and layout fitted to the actual use to which the stand is to be put. The end purpose is too little thought about in the design of stands. But in reality your stand is a stage set for the particular production that you and your staff are going to mount.

Will there be a circulation plan within your stand or will visitors be left to wander about as they want? Whatever your answer, make certain that the decision is visitor-orientated and not just a way of making life easier for you and your designer. Your job is to attract visitors to your exhibits, to the goods you are selling, not to the construction which surrounds them, and a glance at any exhibition will show you how hard this is to achieve. You are selling your company, your products and your ideas. If the stand doesn't do this, the whole thing will have been an expensive mistake.

Lastly, when the content and communication of your message and the way circulation is to be handled have all been settled, your designer must check that he has not left out any basic housekeeping elements: space for secure storage of coats and bags for your staff (and for your visitors as well); space for storage of publications, forms and all the other literature you will be using; office facilities, phones, telex terminals; kitchen facilities and perhaps an adjacent food and drink store; adequate seating; all these are typical examples. There is a checklist in Part Three to help you identify them, for they all have to be fitted into the organised jigsaw of the stand in such a way that they do not intrude into its central purpose of sales and promotion.

SCRIPTWRITING AND GRAPHICS

Special factors in scriptwriting

Preparing the script for an exhibition is one of the most difficult forms of script writing. The result must be accurate; it must be succinct; it must be to the point; and beyond all these it must actively invite the visitor to read it. Your script is in direct competition with your neighbours', and it has to be finely tuned to the particular clientele at which your whole marketing and exhibition strategy is directed.

Never let anyone walk onto your stand when it is empty.

However, once the script is agreed, you have not only the basic material for your designer to work on but also the draft text for your press notice and the description of the exhibit for the organisers' exhibition catalogue.

The layout of the words needs as much care as their content. Some people will want to 'fast track' through your text, and will need overall simple headings so that just by reading these they will be able, as they walk by your stand, to grasp and remember your message. The main message these headings convey is designed to attract the passer-by onto your stand to read the secondary message, and this in turn should persuade him to read the detailed information and to respond favourably to your sales staff approach. But keep the detailed information within bounds. Few people will want to sit or, worse, stand reading great tracts of text at an exhibition. Better to make the real detail available in leaflets which the visitor can take away.

In preparing the final text it is useful to note in a column alongside the text each exhibit or illustration which will be accompanying the paragraphs in sequence. If you follow this practice you should end up with a complete resumé of the stand's content.

Remember that if you have interesting products, you should always put a sign above the level of people watching. Messages to fast-track visitors can be equally important.

In order to get near enough to see what interests everybody here you have to move people aside.

A useful stand number box which serves the additional purpose of recording visitors' information.

Drafting the script

Your aim will be simplicity, but before you get it right your text will go through a number of drafts. Be warned here, though: the original good intentions of a clear and simple message may get submerged under the load of comments by other people involved, along with consequent revisions and approvals. Be prepared to re-write the whole thing once everyone has had the chance to comment. The final version needs approval not only from you and your designer but also from your technical staff, though they must save displays of their expertise for the technical press; here they are checking only for factual accuracy. The information you want the visitor to take away must be quickly and easily grasped, so the message must be simple and logical. If it isn't, it will end up as mere patterns of texture on the wall.

If you want to show products on a plinth, allow plenty of opportunity for visitors to get in amongst the exhibits.

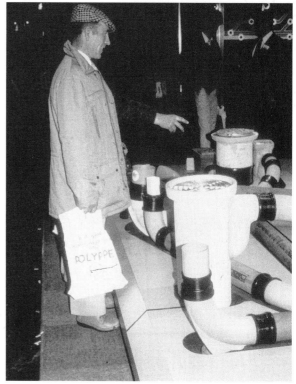

Marketing is not about drinks and refreshments. Unless these are being offered to every visitor, make sure they are invisible during opening hours.

Words and images

Words are not the only or necessarily the best medium for your message. It is often better to integrate them in a diagram or to use illustrations instead. But everything – words, illustrations, photographs, diagrams, maps, exhibits – must work together. Production of script and graphics is therefore a complex task; leave plenty of time for it. With a large and complicated stand you may need to go beyond your designer to a special exhibit script writer, but if you do you must make sure that he has exhibition experience. Having written for television, radio or the press is by no means necessarily an appropriate preparation for this peculiarly difficult job.

Unlike most of the other contributors to your script your designer will be used to thinking in terms not of words only but of integrated text and images, and it is up to him to bring about a happy marriage of word and image. Don't be afraid to keep developing the script right up to the moment the artwork has to be produced, but at the final stage one single person must make sure it still all hangs together and adds up to a coherent and clear message.

When you as client have lived with the prospect for weeks it is all too easy to consider that one main display of your company's name is enough, especially if you have a shell scheme stand provided by the organiser. But it is not. Great crowds of people visit the exhibition, there is a large number of stands and displays, and the visitor often finds it hard to remember what stand he is on. You cannot repeat the corporate identity of your individual stand too often.

It will be no use trying, at the last minute of assembly, to use those lovely blue letters you ordered if the organiser insists on dark green – which may by bad luck be your main competitor's corporate colour. Hall signposting, too, may create problems if you find a large sign right in front of your stand directing people to the restaurants or, worse, the toilets, or, worst, the exit. Your designer must be alert to these possibilities, and must check with the organisers before your exhibit arrives on site.

Graphics

Simplicity is the keynote not only in the choice of words but also in the way they are graphically presented. Your visitor may be in a condition of

Use every opportunity to invite potential visitors onto the stand and don't keep them in the gangway unless you want to make sure they stay there.

near-shellshock from having already passed forty or fifty stands. He may be in no state to tackle anything but a simply presented message in which size and style of lettering, colour, position on stand, the whole graphical pattern, all cohere, both with one another and with the overall design of your stand. Graphics, layout, structure must be designed as one.

The visitor does not want to have to hunt for information. The message on the wall panels, in the form of the exhibits and in the information leaflets must work together in a well thought out sequence. This is another reason for stressing the need to tackle the circulation problem. The exhibition is a sales tool in which the graphics play as important a role as the stand itself, and you must think out the whole sequence of how the visitor approaches and comes onto your stand, examines your exhibits, talks with your staff and departs, if not leaving an order behind, at least bearing away a package or a clear memory which will lead to orders in the future.

Reproducing the graphics

Most people think of typesetting the graphics and reproducing them in some form on wall panels. But there are other techniques, ranging from reproducing handwriting (if it is legible) to ambitious artistic work. Murals painted by a specially commissioned artist may be your main feature. Or a signwriter may handwrite the message onto the panels or walls. If so, make sure you have a back-up in case he gets ill, since the job is being done on site. He will need a union card to work on site, as will your mural painter. The latter is normally employed on a contract separate from that of the main contractor; otherwise you will have to pay the main contractor 10 or 15% for the honour of employing your artist.

There are four main ways of reproducing the graphics on your stand:

1 Photographically, normally on photographic paper, then wet or dry mounted.

2 Signwritten by hand – usually possible only for main headings owing to the time it takes and the consequent cost.

3 Self-adhesive or other applied cut-out letters – excellent for titles and headings but again not easily used if you are putting fifty or more words on a panel.

4 Silkscreen printing. Like the photographic method, usually done for artwork. An excellent way of producing text although it has size limitations due to the maximum practical size of the silkscreen frame.

Beyond these main methods you can also use stencilling, transfers and photocopy enlargements of typescript. There may be problems, particularly of colour, with some of the methods, but given ingenuity and experience almost anything is possible.

Your designer should specify to the contractor exactly who should produce and apply the graphics, usually a job for specialists. Incidentally, all kinds of mistakes may creep in between the marking up of the script for the typesetter and the finished job. Get

One of our friendly exhibitors agreed to pose in this classic position. It is known as the 'Keep off' pose and will deter all but the most determined visitor. If you remember to look away as visitors approach, you can be certain they won't come on your stand.

someone else to proofread the latter; your designer and you will be much too familiar with the text by then to be likely to spot small mistakes. But, depend on it, these will be picked up by your very first visitor. Similarly, all the artwork should be checked by someone else before you initial your approval for the contractor. Mistakes on site are expensive to correct and may be impossible to put right at the last minute.

If the graphics are going to be in place for more than a few days, it is wise to protect them, especially if they are photographically produced, by having them lacquer-varnished or heat-sealed with a plastic overlay film. If so, best to use a matt surface film or finish as this will not reflect the lighting and set up uncomfortable glare for the reader.

Readability can be much helped by the angles at which you set your text panels. Research into average human viewing angles shows that it is much more normal to look down and ahead rather than up and ahead though there is often a conflict to be resolved between the need to keep messages at a reasonable height and the obstruction of them by your staff and your visitors, however welcome. This is something which your designer will keep in mind and something, also, which underlines the need for statements of your company's identity at lower levels than that of the stand fascia. Overall, the way the graphics are used is about the most important element of really good stand design. Indeed, exhibition design has often been called 'three-dimensional graphics'.

10 Construction Costs and Materials

Construction costs can soon run away with you. Do you really need a temporary palace to sell your product? In Britain in the 1950s architect-designed palaces were fashionable at major exhibitions, but few are to be found today unless for some special reason – for example a stand which itself incorporates elements of the building materials being displayed, or one which provides a great deal of office accommodation or meeting room and demonstration space. The economic climate has persuaded us to put our money into a direct selling job rather than a display of prestige building. All the same, it can hardly be denied that in design terms modern exhibitions are duller places for the comparative lack of architects' involvement. They know the economic facts of life as well as the rest of us, and if you make use of their imagination and their special skills they may well achieve for you a stand that is both effective and memorable.

SHELL SCHEMES

The increasing availability of structural systems, with the consequent development of shell scheme structures, hired out by the organisers for each event, has brought about a major change in stand construction. Shell schemes (described in more detail in the opening section of this book) usually consist of side and rear walls or dividers, floor coverings (often of a standard colour throughout the hall), an identification sign (often including your stand number), and some basic lighting.

They are an inexpensive way of participating in an exhibition, but they have some inbuilt disadvantages, chief among which is the sheer boredom for the visitor of walking past a hundred and one virtually identical units. Careful planning can produce for you a much more exciting layout with no loss of space, but this happens all too rarely.

If you do book a shell scheme, try to give it something which will distinguish it from its neighbours. A careful use of colour will often help. Despite the standard colour of carpet and walls or curtains it may not cost much to have your stand a different colour, so long as you arrange it with the organisers early on. And you must check with them, too, about any panels or exhibit fixings which you want to secure to the shell structure; the units are used over and over again and holes in panels, or other damage, could land you with an invoice from the organisers for the replacement of an entire panel.

American and British techniques

Many exhibition organisers in America provide their shell scheme booths with cutaway side walls, and they have additional height restrictions on exhibit material placed forward to the gangway from the point where the side walls or curtains drop in level. This should be clearly stated in the organisers' manual for participants, but your designer must check. He must bear in mind too that most American stands are sold in fixed unit sizes which cannot usually be varied except in exact multiples of the basic unit.

American shell scheme systems are usually created by using curtains or drapes supported on a basic scaffold system, and carpeting normally stuck down with tape direct to the exhibition hall floor. This is often the pattern also in the Middle and Far East and in Australasia. In Britain and in Europe generally the system is more construction-orientated, and often involves a 4 inch high wooden platform to allow cables and other services to be run under it since our older halls lack underfloor electrical wiring. Here stock panels are used, that is to say sheet material, usually of plywood framed up with timber, to create standard panels which are then bolted or screwed together to make the walls; and our booths have a ceiling of stretched fabric.

Never leave visiting cards, your filing tray and your list of contents where they can be seen or borrowed by passing visitors.

If you have a looseleaf order book, don't leave it around for other people to finger through.

It's very difficult to keep control of books intended for sale if they are easily accessible to the passing visitor.

Don't allow any parts of your stand to remain unfinished at any time when the public are in the exhibition.

Commercial systems

In the last few years a number of commercial systems such as *Octanorm* (West Germany) and *Click* (UK) have made their appearance. These can be put together very quickly to provide a well designed shell scheme throughout the hall. But they are much harder to make fixings to. The panels are laminated, and a 6 inch nail driven through one will result in your getting a considerable bill for its replacement. They are also more limited in colours than the normal British stock panels. These can be painted any colour you like, but a laminated panel restricts you to the colour of the lamination originally provided. They may be a different colour on each side, but this hardly offers you much scope to create a brightly coloured stand. It is sometimes possible to get the contractor who is supplying the system to apply a film over the panels, but this is expensive.

THE WORKFORCE

You must be clear about what trades are readily available in the exhibition hall. Normally there are carpenters (assisted by labourers), painters and decorators, electricians and carpet layers. All will be members of unions, often of sections of unions peculiar to the exhibition industry, and they will be working in different groups. For instance, there will be quite a big workforce building the shell scheme itself, and though this is usually scheduled for completion before exhibitors are allowed to begin their work such is not always the case, and problems may arise over the shell scheme workforce getting in the way of your own.

Never use non-union labour in any capacity if you do not want to risk the entire exhibition grinding to a halt. Everyone working on site must have a union card. This includes your own staff, who mustn't touch a screwdriver or re-position an exhibit without clearing with the contractor that they are not contravening any site regulations or union requirements. It includes also, as we have said, any more specialist workmen or artists; they too have to meet union regulations and you must check this with the contractor or exhibition organiser. There is a standard union agreement in the United Kingdom between the exhibition unions and the contractors, and similar agreements are in force in America and across the world.

Visitors as well as exhibitor staff have a bad habit of leaving their hats, coats and bags on your stand. Make sure you know where the cloakroom is.

FIRE AND SAFETY REGULATIONS

All materials used in exhibition construction have to meet stringent fire regulations. These vary from country to country and often from city to city. Details are always available from the organisers. Some of the toughest are those in force in London. In essence, if a material catches fire readily, holds flame and burns easily it cannot be used in any exhibition halls unless it can be satisfactorily fireproofed.

In addition, the local authority surveyor has to approve the structure of any exhibition stand. With a shell scheme the organiser will obtain blanket approval, and this normally covers fire approvals as well, but any additional panels or exhibit you use will also have to meet the regulations. If you have exhibits which create a safety hazard you will need special approval under, for example, the regulations covering protection of visitors from moving machinery. Your designer must get all necessary approvals before you appear on site. If he doesn't get them, you probably won't open for business on time.

It is useful to have a signwriter around on opening day, but if he has to correct spelling or add some vital signs, try to give him adequate workspace in your office, not at the front of your stand.

If you haven't ordered enough panels, plinths or wall shelves for a complete range of exhibits, don't put them on the floor where they might be especially dangerous to visitors backing off your stand.

OPEN-AIR EXHIBITIONS

Open-air exhibitions – Agricultural Shows, State Fairs and the like – are a different matter. Many regular exhibitors at this kind of show provide themselves with exhibits based on caravan, bus or truck chassis. All they need to do is drive on to their site, park and set up, connecting to the services available, and get straight on with selling. The essential is to make sure that your display is secure and proof against the elements, especially rain (or worse) and wind, but against direct sunlight too if you are using colour photographs or other material sensitive to the light.

THE USE OF PLASTICS

Construction materials are many and various. Most basic work is in timber and metal, with fabric, glass and floor coverings and the commonest support materials. Plastics are not widely used because of fire problems. Unlike traditional fabric, sheet plastic is almost impossible to fireproof unless this characteristic is built into it on manufacture. Rigid plastics such as acrylics (Perspex, Oroglass etc.) are usually banned completely except for very small scale use in cut-out lettering. Foam plastics, particularly rigid polystyrenes, are acceptable only if they are of the fire-retardant variety. Some countries do not allow these materials, and their exclusion is a blow to the designer since they lend themselves so well to creative design; but the fire officers' case is very compelling.

SOLVING THE LOAD PROBLEM

You will have to make special arrangements if your stand involves the display of extra heavy or large loads. Checks must be made with the hall owners to

It is very important not to let the stand get that 'lived-in' look, from being filled up with other peoples' luggage.

The floor is never the place for literature, postcards or other material you hope visitors will use.

establish access and floor loading limits, and specialist movers may need to be employed. In a number of countries, including America, the unions have an agreement that one particular contractor must be used for all movement of materials or exhibits within the hall; the exhibitor may ship to the door but the contractor will take it from there. In Europe there is genenerally an 'official' contractor recognised by the organisers, but no actual ban on others carrying out the work provided they are qualified and insured.

Your heavy exhibits will often have to be moved into position before shell schemes or neighbouring stands are constructed, so be ready to ship them early. You must inform the organisers about this from the start so that they can programme both delivery and removal into their setting-up and break-down schedules. Remember that you will need to provide protective covers for your exhibits – and even 24-hour security guards if the item in question is your latest model, to be unveiled on opening day!

The weight problem on site can often be overcome by spreading the load, which can be achieved by introducing a one inch (25mm) sheet of blockboard under the heavy object. Building bricks, or a suitable thickness of steel plate, can often provide useful support below the 4 inch (100mm) platforms of European exhibition stands. But it is very unwise to rely on do-it-yourself solutions.

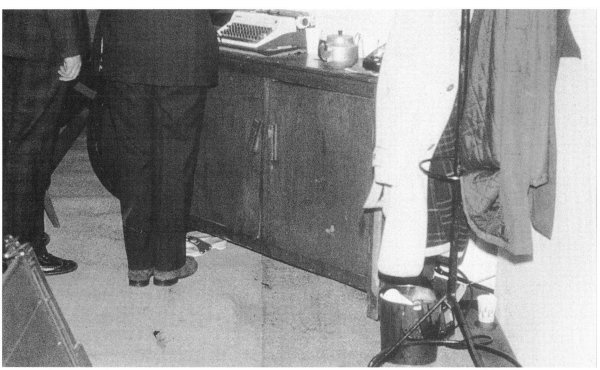

Waste paper baskets should never be full; and if you must have a coat rack on your stand try to keep it away from the main viewpoint where it will cover up any messages.

You can't get at this literature without crawling on the floor.

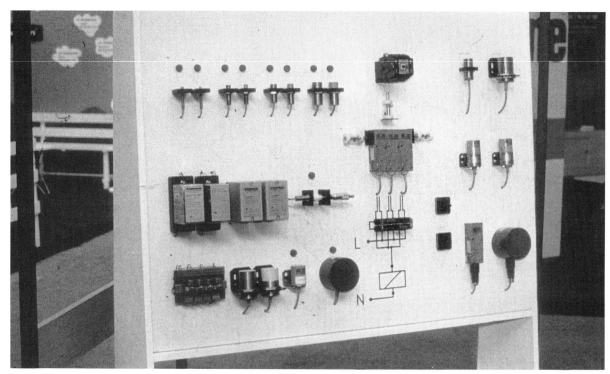

A very well-designed panel containing interesting products, but with no name of company or indication of special interest to the visitor.

Free-standing panels are useful for displaying information, but always try to include the name of the company, or its logo, or basic information for the casual visitor.

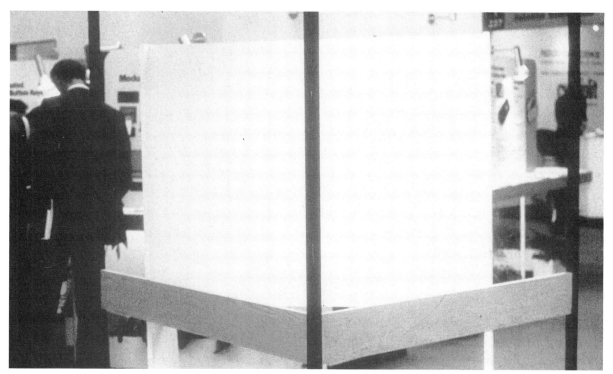

White space is wasted space.

Your designer must ask a qualified structural engineer for the simplest solution to any weight problems on your stand.

Similar problems in transporting your exhibit across the hall to your stand must be separately resolved with the organisers and, through them, the hall owners. You may also need a high voltage cable, or compressed air or gas, to work a machine on your stand, and all these requirements must be requested from the organisers as soon as possible. In all problems of this kind the organisers are the best point of contact for your designer.

FIXINGS

Most fixings used in the exhibition industry are of a temporary nature and as easily dismantled as they are fixed. Much of the shell scheme systems snap, lock, slide or bolt together; carpeting and floor covering is nearly always laid using removable double-headed tape; and some materials, such as the casement fabric used for many European ceilings, are so cheap that they are used once and thrown away.

Mechanical fixing – nailing, screwing, stapling – involves attaching the objects one to another by physically connecting them with metal or plastic connectors. Adhesive fixings, which usually come in the form of liquid or semi-liquid glues or of adhesive tapes, are viewed with distrust by many exhibition workmen, especially by carpenters, but they can still be extremely useful. The designer will be wise, however, to check with the manufacturer or with his contractor friends before specifying a particular adhesive.

Also available are one or two other fixing methods. There is the 'Velcro' fabric system and various types of double-sided adhesive tape. These can be used for attaching lightweight exhibits, photographs and captions to the stand walls.

There is also a hidden support system for panels which is used almost universally in exhibition construction – split battens. These are two pieces of wood, each with one angled edge. One is fixed to the panel, the other to the wall, and the panel is then simply dropped down over the wall batten. If the battens are cut shorter than the panel width and centred, the panel to which they are applied appears to be floating. But whatever methods of fixing you use, you must make sure that they are secure.

We have already spoken of the need to conform to

*Flowers enhance many stands, but don't let them get in
the way of the product.*

Two useful wall panels but no information for the passing visitor.

regulations. If you want to support some part of your display, perhaps a hanging sign, from the hall structure, particularly by means of cable from the roof, you will have to get special permission from the hall owners as well as from the structural engineers of both the hall and the local authority. Often this will not be allowed since many roofs have no tolerance for additional point loadings, but even if it is, safety aspects will probably lead the local authority to insist on two independent means of support in case one fails – for instance, cables and safety chains. This belt-and-braces requirement relates not only to large structures but also to individual lights supported over publicly accessible areas, and equally to aspects of your own exhibits; unsupported crane jibs for example may not be allowed unless they are so located that if they did collapse no harm would be done.

You will certainly have to pay a great deal for using support from the roof, not least because most halls have very high roof structures and the riggers who erect such items are very expert, very highly insured and very highly paid. But it may well be worth going to this extra trouble to create a better display than your competitor, who may not bother. This may be the only way to get your machines actively working and not static, if power cabling can only be brought onto your stand from the roof.

FINISHES

The main criteria for wall and other finishes are ease of use in design and the ability to keep a pristine appearance right up to the closing day.

Paints
For this reason designers often use easily replaceable finishes such as emulsion paint, which can be re-painted every night if needs be. Matt finish plastic emulsion paint forms an ideal finish for skirtings, platform edgings and other surfaces which may be easily damaged.

Vinyls
Much used also for wall finishes are vinyls and washable wallpaper since they often work out

*Flowers should not be an afterthought and should not be
used to fill empty spaces or to hide chairs.*

ABOVE   *A well-designed use of light in the step riser so that there can be no excuse for not noticing the change of height.*

LEFT   *A good example of seeing a product in use, but those sharp edges might be dangerous if they are at knee height adjoining the gangway.*

This stand is very closed in but the products may demand that the casual visitor can't see what's on show.

A clear example of good product board captioning, but it would mean nothing to the casual visitor giving the stand a quick glance. The top main headline should always be aimed at the fast track visitor.

Outdoor sites with machinery are much easier for designers to work on. They really only need sign-posting and the stand size to be clearly marked.

Stand edges on green field exhibition sites can easily be marked with a post and chain.

ABOVE   *Product identification outdoors is very easy because a simple post stuck in the grass is not only adjustable but can be changed for different products at different times of the day.*

If you are staging a working demonstration, make sure you have plenty of room. It would also be an advantage to have a sign simulating a load to advertise the product to the casual visitor.

If your concrete mixer is indoors, make sure it has good signs identifying its main advantages.

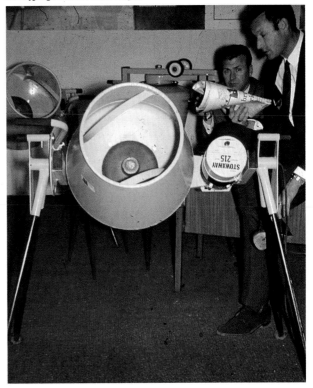

People always like to see demonstrations, particularly if, for example, they can cut bricks themselves. Make sure however, that your stand does not become like a building site filled with too-enthusiastic groups of demonstrators.

Clear signposting of a stand is essential but it is also useful to remember that casual visitors don't always know what your company makes — and casual visitors may well one day turn into useful contacts.

A good example of a leaflet rack which allows self-service, for a product where you don't necessarily need to know the name of every person who has shown interest.

LEFT *A good example of a clear sign, attractive to every visitor, with a good competition that will attract the crowds.*

BELOW *A good example of very clear posting of a name — over the entrance so that it is easy to see how to get onto the stand. Lampshades can be dangerous when left swinging near the gangway and these are clearly contained from passing visitors.*

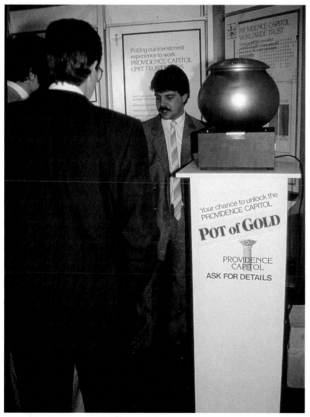

This gold vase is certainly a great prize. It is at a good height for attracting casual visitors and will excite people's curiosity.

An excellent example of a product caption, clearly showing its name and its unique advantage.

for quality foundry m[...]
consult
BALBARDIE.....
Always available
Low in cost
Better castings
After sales service
Reduction in scrap
Double-quick delivery
Improved surface fini[...]
Economic in use

If people are to be moved or pointed in a certain direction, the arrows and signs can't be too big.

LEFT *Verbal games are often popular. This is a good example of the letters of a company name being used, to provide the initial letter of each of the unique advantages it is claiming.*

Where models of buildings or products are shown, the use of over-bright colours and unusual shapes always attracts attention.

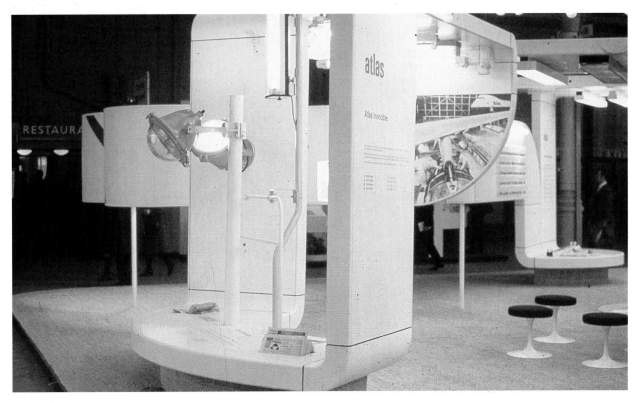

A good example of a free-standing design allowing products to be individually collected and displayed, but which also permits maximum use of the stand to attract attention from all directions.

LEFT   *Machines which move at exhibitions always need fencing off for safety and to stop too-curious people getting in the way.*

Some machines are so complicated that the addition of signs, arrows and descriptive notes would be helpful.

A clear sign with two messages, but neither of them are particularly relevant to the machine from the user's point of view. Also, try to put the fire extinguisher where the exhibitor can use it and don't hang hats and coats on the end of your machines.

A seemingly haphazard display can often be an attraction in its own right.

If the gangways are small and dense, try to lift up your product so that everyone can see it without its being confused with the crowds.

*An interesting example of the use of flowers: a moat filled
with water and a solid glass wall are used to direct
visitors to very limited access.*

cheaper on large wall surfaces than the more traditional paint finishes, which may require two or three coats before a successful finish is achieved. As well as for their cost effectiveness they are chosen for their ease of cleaning. They should be wrap-mounted wherever possible so that edges between rolls do not look unsightly.

Melamine

Suppliers of melamine sheets for shell schemes have self-adhesive film available which can be added to the white surface to give colour. Colours are usually bright and need using with care. They will have to be agreed with the organisers and ordered early on by them from the shell scheme contractor. He will almost certainly apply the film before he comes on site and invoice you direct for this extra work. As always, get a written quotation before you order, and make sure that your designer goes on site to see that all is well before the shell scheme contractor leaves (which is usually before your own contractor is allowed on site). It would be expensive if you had to call his men back, and impossible if they had gone off to work in another hall.

Carpets

The quality of carpet you choose will depend on how long the exhibition is to run; but remember that most shell schemes include the floor covering. Carpet tiles are a sensible choice, so that if some disaster occurs a few replaced tiles will restore everything to its original splendour. When you order them, don't forget to order those extra emergency ones at the same time so that they all come from the same manufactured batch.

If you are a regular or frequent exhibitor or if you are a member of a large group, consider buying some standard-sized carpet tiles in your own corporate colour and with your logo or name cut out and set in each tile. You will often be able to include some in your shell stand flooring or add them to your own scheme. They add enormously to the personality of your stand.

Ceilings

Stand ceilings can take almost any form. The most popular are modular suspended ceiling structures or those made of stretched fabric.

The main fabric used is a specially fireproofed cotton casement cloth which is usually available in a good range of colours. Again, if you are in a shell

scheme and want any colour other than white, you must order this through the organiser early on. Be careful that when the hall lights are on or natural daylight is coming through, the ceiling colour does not throw an unwanted colour cast over everything. A cheaper fabric, also available in many colours but more transparent, is muslin; and if you are located partly under a gallery or stair where cigarette ends may land on your roof you will need glass silk cloth.

More expensive but still a very cheap way of creating dark areas, unaffected by the wall lights, is bolton cloth. Remembered in its black-dyed form as wartime 'blackout' material, it hangs extremely well as curtains and is lightproof. It is usually available in only about eight colours, but you can extend your colour possibilities by using white bolton cloth on top of a coloured casement cloth.

The ceiling fabrics we have mentioned so far are normally stretched as great flat expanses. But

If you are selling flowers or flower boxes by all means make a good display.

splendid effects can be achieved with coloured casements and muslins gathered, tucked and pleated into ceiling designs. These 'velaria' designs, all the rage in the past, are not much used today and, like many such 'old' techniques, should be revived.

Any normal finish can be used for solid ceilings, although decorative stretched fabric could provide a good detail finish, and some form of *trompe l'oeil* surface decoration could be applied, by hand or photographically. Lighting, which is dealt with later, can provide striking effects, especially of movement such as clouds rushing across. Barriers and louvres can work well; both can carry additional company or product information, and they can even stretch right down to the floor to divide up your stand space.

THE VIEW FROM ABOVE

When you are designing your ceiling details, make sure that any views from surrounding galleries do not expose all the structural and electrical clobber. This top space should be used to identify the stand to visitors looking over the hall from above. The commonest problem of potential visitors is that they simply fail to find your stand, and the view from above is (or can be, for the opportunity is often missed) extremely helpful in pinpointing your location in the hall.

KEEPING THE STAND FRESH

Laminated plastics are much used for counters, desks and shelves, for whilst they are expensive they reduce site work to a minimum and wear very well indeed. All reduction of site work is to be strongly encouraged as it costs about twice as much to keep the workforce on site as it does to use them at their own premises.

In detailing the stand for tendering, the designer's special concern should be with the way all finishes are 'finished' at corners, junctions, and other points where changes of material occur. If this work is well done it will do more than anything else to ensure that the stand stays in pristine condition throughout the exhibition.

QUICK ASSEMBLY DISPLAYS

Your concern may not be with heavy objects at all but may range, according to the size of your exhibit, right across the spectrum down to the suitcase displays discussed earlier.

Small shell scheme booths are often booked by companies which bring their own exhibition panel system with them, slot it together on site and open for business. Most organisers have 'official' furniture hirers who will arrange to supply you with tables, chairs, portable bars, refrigerators – provided you have ordered them in time.

Whether your small-scale exhibit uses display panels which come from a van, from the back of your car or from a suitcase, there are currently available many attractive and sophisticated systems which will grace most halls or hotel venues. But whatever you construct, large or small, do make sure that every bit is earning money for you, even if only indirectly in goodwill, prestige and reputation.

11 Power, Lighting and Audio-Visuals

THE POWER SUPPLY

Organising the power supply

Your designer will have to work at the stand's electrical requirements early on so that the organisers can supply what is needed. This is particularly important if you are going to require unusual loadings like four-phase to operate your machines. Again, the organiser will need to know early on if you want to add to (or have your own special location needs for) the basic lights which come as part of the shell scheme package.

Power supply to your stand is normally via your own meter and switchboard which is hired to you for the duration of the show by the nominated 'official' electricians. The organisers may well require a deposit both on the equipment and on the supply of power since, unhappily, exhibitors sometimes forget or delay paying their electricity and telecommunications invoices at the end of the show. Telephones, telex, facsimile machines and even computer modem lines, as well as photocopiers, typewriters and word processors, can be hired in much the same way. Many service contractors will even supply office staff to man these facilities, although it is usually better to use your own staff, who are already familiar with your business and know the people working in it.

Estimating the power supply

How do you work out the power you need? This is just a question of adding up the various wattages of the total setup and remembering that 1000 watts = 1 kilowatt (a kilojoule in metric terms). Most display spots or flood lamps normally rate 100 or 150 watts, fluorescent lamps much less (probably 30 to 60 watts), and each 13 amp socket outlet at full use could, though rarely does, consume up to 2 kilowatts.

An excellent example of a firm that is not afraid to reproduce its name as often as possible. This is a good use of a fascia for the fast-track visitor.

A clear understanding of the use of the logo, the company name and detailed product captioning. All these signs can be read by visitors approaching and passing at different speeds. There is clear uninterrupted access onto the stand for the visitor who wants to know more information.

A good example of a nameboard giving different information about products, with the appropriate literature dispenser underneath.

When you work out the power supply you must not forget all the little extra items such as power sockets for the coffee machine, the refrigerator, the air conditioner and the cleaning equipment. It is sometimes better to have double switched sockets fitted as they are often cheaper than two single sockets. A small contingency percentage should be added to the total when the outline lighting scheme has been worked out. This avoids the considerable expense later on of getting more power to site rather than just installing more points or lamps.

Ordering the power supply

For a purpose-built stand the organisers' electrical contractor will want to know only the total loading,

roughly how it divides between light and power and where the main junction box should be located on the stand. For shell schemes they need to know rather more as they may well not be allowed to re-position lights, and a special clip may be used to prevent the shell scheme panels being damaged. Take care that your main switchboard does not end up in a prime visual location or simply hanging by its feed cable in the centre of your back wall. Your designer should issue exact location details to the contractors, and must tell them too that you do not want any visible and damaging fixings made on your parts of the interior display, particularly if you intend to use them elsewhere later on. With shell schemes the scheme's electrical contractors will

A large amount of fascia space not being used: the only signs and the only information about the stand are in small type and on one wall.

Clear product information and a simple way of keeping people off the stand while still enabling them to approach it from a more limited access.

usually provide the actual fittings as well as the power to run them; otherwise the hire of fittings and their connection are normally part of your contractor's task.

POWERED DISPLAYS

Audio-visual displays

The Exhibitors' Manual issued by the organisers normally contains the forms and deadlines needed for arranging all these various connections. Make sure you get the correct type of line if you need facsimile or computer modem operation. Your decision on whether to have any form of audio-visual display, be it a slide and sound show, video, film or even a mixture, will turn purely on whether it will help to get your message across.

All audio-visual displays are expensive, both in straight cost and in space terms; and the organisers

Machinery needs guarding: this guard rail enables people to see the machinery but keeps them away from dangerous moving parts.

and hall owners, not to mention your neighbouring exhibitors, are understandably not keen on gangways filled with stationary audiences watching your show. Indeed, in many exhibitions film screens have to be so placed that they cannot be seen from the gangways.

Unless you are presenting a full cinema-type show you must not expect audiences to stand and watch for more than about two minutes. And in his design of the stand your designer must never forget that even in this technological age breakdowns occur, equipment fails and screens go blank. Always make sure that you know the location of the AV maintenance crew.

'Hands-on' exhibits

Electrics can be simply used to provide some good 'hands-on' quizzes and games for visitors, which can tell them a lot about your products. Computer games can do the same job in a much more sophisticated way but often take far too long about it, and even mechanical 'hands-on' displays using simple hinged flaps on hand-cranked machines can be great fun and an ideal way to break the ice with a first-time contact.

Holograms and lasers

You may decide to get holograms made of some of your products or to use laser patterns to attract visitors to your stand. If you do, it is essential to employ experts, not least because there are very strict safety regulations governing the use of lasers in public spaces.

KINDS OF LIGHTING

Good lighting will make an exhibit; bad lighting can kill even the best designed stand. Your designer must therefore tackle the matter of lighting from the outset; adding track and trying to solve problems on site almost never work satisfactorily. In introducing track for display lights the lighting industry has ingeniously arranged to sell you not only the fittings but the track as well. But if your designer is clear about where the lights need to go and can locate them on his drawings, the connections can be made with cable, which is much cheaper than track.

Don't rush your decisions but get your designer to sketch out his basic proposals and discuss with him how the effects are to be achieved. The lighting is the most important single factor in making or

This stand appears to have a large amount of wall preventing access but the products can nevertheless be clearly seen by visitors passing on the gangway.

A good example of judicious blending of typescript and product. Complementary use of textures is particularly attractive to passing designers.

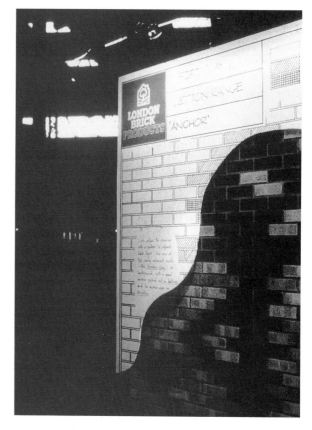

breaking your display. It forms an important and integral part of the stand design, whether you use simple overall good levels of light throughout, or make dramatic use of light to highlight the main points of your story. Moving light sequences can be used to draw visitors on to your stand, possibly with sound accompaniment, and then take them through a sequence of events like a miniature *son et lumière* production.

Unfortunately a great many lights now on the market make no attempt to be more than fancy shapes with bulbs stuck in them, and the trade needs to rethink its attitude towards providing the sort of fittings the professional lighting designer needs. Some of these have taken to manufacturing their own fittings, an expensive recourse for you but worth it if the results are good. Others have returned to using theatrical lighting (usually very expensive on short-life specialist lamps) and to making much more use of very simple lamp holders with suitable hidden locations built into the exhibition stand structure.

The commonest instance of bad lighting is undoubtedly glare from the light source. Are you to have concealed or revealed light fittings? Most professional lighting designers, unless they are producing some kind of lighting feature or indeed a stand for a lighting manufacturer, would opt for the light source to be hidden. This removes distracting glare and helps create the dramatic effect which artificial light provides so well. Remember in creating this effect that if there is intrusive daylight it may well have to be screened off. Sunlight moves during the day and can dramatically change the look of your stand in some halls. In the evening, too, hall lighting can unexpectedly affect your stand's visual appeal.

There are many different kinds of light source, and the most common, with their basic characteristics, are listed in the attached charts. The recent ranges which are based on low-voltage lamps can be very tiny and are useful for detailed highlighting. Don't forget that you can add colour, accurate light patterning and simple movement, and even control shutters and barn doors.

POWER FOR HEAVY EXHIBITS

In touching earlier on the problems of extra-heavy machinery on your stand, we mentioned that you might need to order a special power supply to run such items. First you must make sure that the floor of the hall can take the loadings and possible vibrations. If so, you must then specify the exact feed you require. This can usually be provided, though high loadings may not be available in some halls or some countries. If there are a great number of displays operating heavy machines like those for work stations, sheers and presses or plastics extrusion machinery, the organisers may require you to schedule your morning start-up time and to limit the frequency and phase the timings of your demonstrations. Few exhibition halls have the electrical capability of custom-built operating factories.

You must specify AC (Alternating Current) or DC (Direct Current), number of phases, cycles and the actual voltage required. The level of supply, to say nothing of its quality and constancy, varies greatly around the world. The listing on p. 157 gives some idea of the standard variation, which may alter from place to place as well as from country to country. Indeed, a modern exhibition hall may have its own power plant, with its own variation and idiosyncrasies.

Whenever the power is due to be switched on,

make sure that your stand main switches are off. There may be a power surge at this point, which can very effectively wreck a great deal of equipment, especially audio-visual gear and computer controls.

TELEPHONE LINES

The ordering of telephone lines is something your designer is often unable to do for you, especially in Britain, for the national supplier will accept orders only from those who are to pay the final invoices and take direct responsibility for the equipment and its use. There should be no problem over lines for basic systems such as standard phones and telex though they must be ordered in good time; information on the date will be found in the Exhibitors' Manual. You will need special arrangements for satellite TV links, high capacity TV aerials, modem lines for links to off-site computers, facsimile machine line and permanently open private telephone lines back to your offices; and you should start enquiries with the local telecommunications supplier at the earliest opportunity. Incidentally, backup items such as photocopiers can usually be hired locally, as can most post office machinery and even sometimes small computers.

VIDEO

Until recently most programming in the United Kingdom of audio-visual equipment, particularly video, has been with video tape in VCR (Video Cassette Recorder), VHS (Video Home System) or BETAMAX, all of them systems developed on half-inch tape for the UK home video trade. The UMATIC system is based on three-quarter inch tape. Of much higher quality, it is widely used for industrial video productions.

Video discs are now available, resembling gramophone records but scanned by a laser. They are much more expensive but last much longer and have the capacity to carry massive amounts of information. Their other great advantage over tape is that they do not need to re-wind to return to the beginning of an audio-visual programme, leaving a blank screen in the process.

All video discs are essentially 'copies', made by a high-tech development of the method used to make long-playing records; they are in effect 'stamped out'. The big difference from records is that since there is no contact between pickup and disc there is

A stand open on two frontages, with the products displayed on walls across the centre of the stand, provides useful office space behind the stand for private meetings. Nevertheless, there should always be room for representatives to remain on the stand and talk to visitors.

To have the actual product on display and photographs showing where it can be used is a good use of a visual opportunity. However, the prominence given to numbers is not going to be helpful to passing visitors.

no disc wear. In theory therefore a disc lasts for ever, though careless handling may in practice prevent this.

If you are exhibiting overseas the different television systems in use may cause problems with video equipment. America, Canada and Japan have the NISC system, France, USSR and most of Eastern Europe the SECAM system. Nearly everywhere else the PAL system is in use. There are also minor differences in some national systems. Multistandard systems are available but you must in that event make sure that the video player and the TV are both multistandard.

Until recently, getting a good-size, high quality picture has presented problems. Only 26 inch screens (these are always measured on the diagonal) have normally been available. Today, however, there are good systems which project large cinema pictures; and the latest development is a system which can split images across a 'wall' of monitors. Both these effects can be either bought or hired, and to achieve optimum results from their use programme production will need to be of top broadcasting quality. Computer graphics have also been developed recently, but this still tends to be very costly and is not yet normally competitive with hand-produced graphics.

SLIDES

Other audio-visual media to be considered are slides and film. All the show equipment for either can be hired as well as bought outright. Slides are likely to be the cheapest method available to you, and they give the best quality of reproduction as well as being easy to update since individual slides can be readily replaced. But they have an overriding disadvantage in exhibition use: they need re-wind time, and this means blank screens unless you provide another projector to display your company name and logo during the break.

FILM

Film needs to be kept running, so a film loop is often used with the film running over rollers in a storage box. Splices should be minimal and the film needs to be nylon based and specially wax coated. The loop should always be unthreaded and left to hang unfolded by the projector when left overnight or longer.

Exotic systems are also available, most of them extremely sophisticated and using 70mm film. An example is IMAX, also available with a fisheye lens to produce OMNIMAX, which is a 'wrap around' system enveloping the audience in image and multitrack sound. 3D systems also exist, but they usually involve issuing the audience with polarised glasses; and none of these systems is likely to be within the budget of trade show exhibitors.

There is no shortage of specialists and books on audio-visual for further consultation. But remember, whatever you decide on, that the production must be short unless you are providing a full cinema setup with seats and definite showing times. It must not interfere with your other stand activities or make it impossible for your stand staff, or your neighbours' stand staff, to operate satisfactorily.

PROJECTION OF SLIDES AND FILM

There are two main forms of projection. Front projection involves projecting onto an opaque screen, usually with a matt white lenticular (a silver screen like the – no longer used – glass-beaded screen, where the problem was that the glass beads tended to fall off). Perlux (the professional screen used in commercial cinemas) and Daylight Viewing (a very high grain screen made from embossed aluminium) are also ideal for video projection. The difficulty is that all these screens really need cinema darkness conditions and the projection beam can be easily ruined by someone walking in front of it.

The second type is a rear projection screen where the projector is behind the screen (so that you must remember to get the film prints flipped and the slides turned). These screens can be Glass (not just ground or sandblasted but made for the job), Acrylic (dark-tinted and transparent with an applied surface) or Flexible (dark-tinted translucent PVC). The advantages of rear projection are that the image remains good in fairly high ambient light conditions, and that it is much easier to design into an exhibition stand.

As well as standard audio-visual presentations there are also specially adapted slide projectors known as 'random access' which will project any slide from the tray on push-button demand. These

A lot of text to read and it will be necessary to stand on the exhibit to take in all the messages. Nevertheless, people always enjoy seeing comparative arrows giving information about success rates.

If you are looking for an agent, you should give more information about the country or region involved.

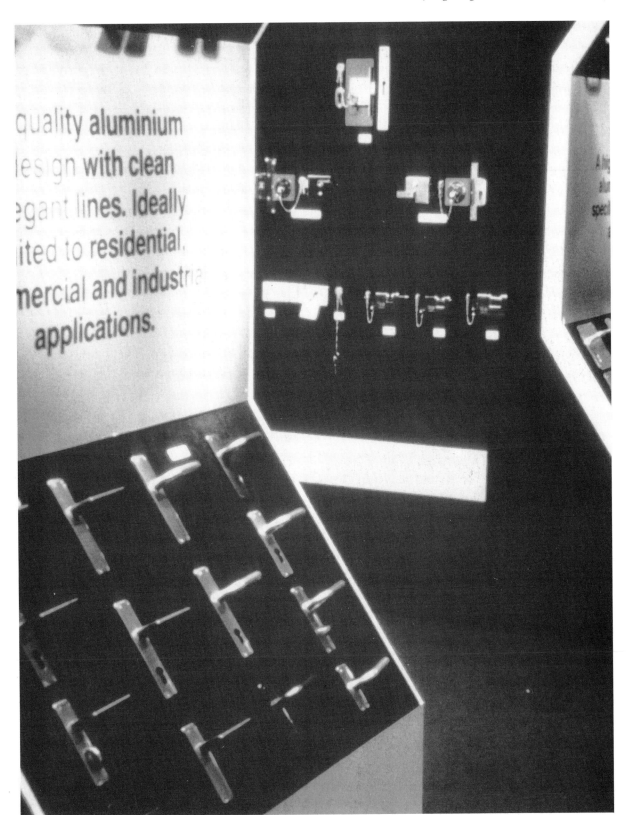

A good example of a simple main sentence for the casual visitor, with more detailed information once you get on the stand.

will also run as normal sequential projectors, with no need for blank screens; and they can be used, too, as an audience 'hands-on' display to introduce your range of products and their uses, or as a staff selling tool. They can even be linked to graphics for a quiz or game.

THE LIFE OF TAPES, FILMS AND SLIDES

Film loops have a special problem since the wear on them is directly proportional to the number of times they pass through the projector rather than to the operating hours, and this in turn obviously depends on the length of the film. If it is kept clean, a good loop system should give 1,500 passes of the film, and some systems claim a lot more. As in the case of all the other media, it should be sufficient to have one set for a one-month exhibition. But with every kind you should have spares available in case of mishap,

---

The benefits of a product are always of interest to visitors, especially where they are simple, clearly spelt out and immediately identifiable.

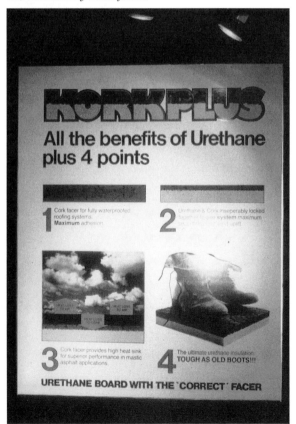

and these should be kept readily accessible but never on the stand itself.

For shows lasting more than a month other factors start to come into play. The life of a tape depends of course on how many times it is used, and this depends in turn on its length. Obviously a ten-minute presentation will have three times as many showings in a given time as will a thirty-minute one. So, if you are running a ten-minute video programme continuously on tape, it is best that the tape itself consists of the same programme six times over so that the machinery has to rewind only once an hour instead of every ten minutes. In a typical continuous running installation we would expect tape or video cassettes to be replaced about every three months.

It is less easy to give advice on slides since the life of any slide depends on how long it is in the gate; if for example, you were to project a single slide continuously without advancing the projector at all you would get noticeable fading after about twenty hours. In practice, when the show is given hourly and a typical slide will be in the gate for only a few seconds, you need only replace them once a year. But if you are showing at something like an Expo Pavilion where you may be running the same slides through the gate four or five times an hour or more, you may need to replace them every three months. Should this create a particular problem, there is special film material available which can give considerably longer life, though at the expense of higher preparation cost.

SOUND

Sound can be a great help on its own or even with light effects. Its volume and direction are very important; remember that hard glossy surfaces reflect sound whilst soft-textured surfaces, particularly carpet or rough fabrics, absorb it and stop it bouncing about. People are also great absorbers of sound. This almost certainly means that you will need to turn the volume up when the stand is crowded and down when it is empty. The normal source of the sound will be an auto-reverse tape machine, usually with a cassette sound tape; and depending on the effect you require, you can use directional, multi-directional, stereo or mini speakers.

COPYRIGHT OF SOUND AND IMAGE

Music, recorded sound, photographs, library film, video – all will be someone's copyright. You must get prior permission for their use and pay the necessary fees. Whatever it costs it is likely to be cheaper than producing your own, and you already know exactly what you are getting.

TWO GOLDEN RULES

It is essential to remember two more things. First, of all the requirements connected with the operation of electrics, lighting and especially audio-visual, the most important is probably having good, quick and reliable maintenance ready to hand if anything goes wrong. Nothing is worse than flashing fluorescent lamps, failed lights or blank projection screens. You must be equipped and ready from the outset to put these things right. If you are hiring your AV equipment from the organisers' official AV contractor, the provision of stand-by maintenance should be a part of your hire contract.

The second golden rule is never to use originals or masters of audio-visual programmes. Use only copies direct from the original master, and remember to order enough to last through the whole show.

One exhibitor who is very much aware that here a purchasing decision depends on identifying the foreman (and very often the machine minder) and selling them the benefits of the machine.

12 Specialist Features, Display Work and Security

WHY YOU NEED FEATURES

At some shows you will be competing with thousands of other exhibitors. The exhibition centre at Dusseldorf, West Germany, for instance, has 13 individual exhibition halls as well as a complete conference centre. You therefore have to find some way of standing out from the crowd. You can do this with an eye-catching feature, a live demonstration, a piece of sculpture (perhaps featuring your product), or simply colour and light. A different approach is to create an 'oasis' in the hurly-burly with seats and plants and moving water. But if you decide to follow this route you will need very careful design and control to make sure you don't become the rest area for the whole hall, with your stand completely blocked and endless sales opportunities lost.

TRADITIONAL FEATURES

Don't dismiss the traditional props such as planting, water effects, flags and banners, and murals. They can still be most effective if they are used as an integral part of the display. But they will not work if they are arbitrarily added later on, so don't allow the Managing Director's wife to practise her flower arranging unless it is a proper part of the display, perhaps in the office area.

It is impossible to cover all the various kinds of features here. They can range from plant tower structures at outside exhibitions such as agricultural shows to delicate and minute displays which nonetheless intrigue and impress visitors by their very nature. The Koh-i-Noor Diamond feature at the 1851 Great Exhibition was relatively tiny; but it drew the crowds.

FINDING YOUR SPECIALIST

Most features have one thing in common: they are best produced by specialist artists and experts and not by your general contractor. So, when you and your designer have settled on what you want but have no one to carry it out for you, how do you find these specialists?

You should not restrict your hunt to the field of commercial exhibition construction. There are, for instance, a number of specialist model makers who produce such items as dioramas, glass-painting and other semi-three-dimensional representation. They often specialise also in modelling products (such as giant tomato ketchup bottles) for television commercials and film props. Indeed the world of theatre design may well be able to provide the person you want.

Specialist manufacturers and experts in flags, banners, stretched fabric and similar features can be found in the Yellow Pages and other directories, as can plant experts and audio-visual producers. There are some amazing talents about; they just need finding. You may want something really out of the ordinary – perhaps you are a brick manufacturer and want an avant-garde brick sculpture: then your only course is really to keep your eyes open, to visit art galleries and generally to ask around. Your designer should certainly be able to help. And don't forget that the person you want may have done a press advertisement for your advertising agents, so have a word with their creative people too.

BRIEFING AND WORKING WITH YOUR SPECIALIST

Once you have found your artist it is imperative that your designer gives him a written brief outlining the main elements and objectives of your requirements. The ideas, the volume of space, the proposed

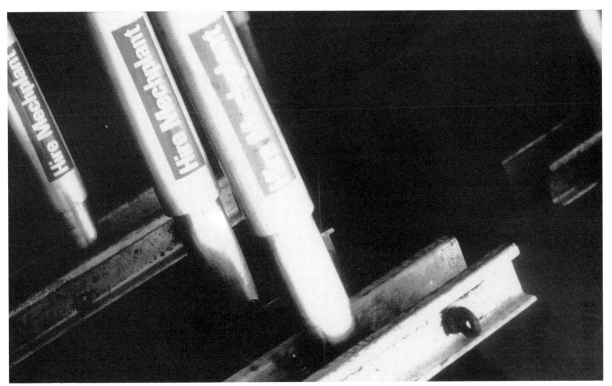

It is a good idea to know what you can hire out as well as what you can sell, but a message of this kind doesn't necessarily need repeating.

Despite the oblique angle of the visitor the type is large enough and the sentences short enough to maintain impact.

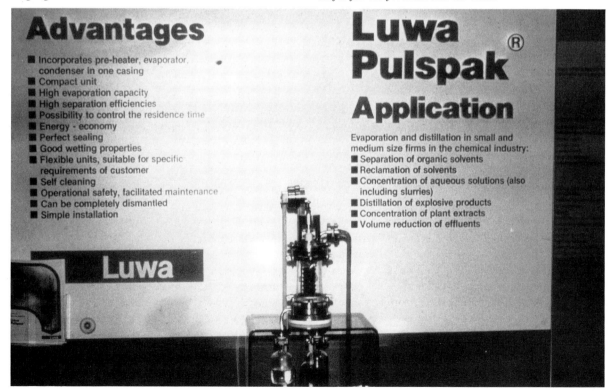

Multi-lingual messages are always difficult because of the imbalance of the number of words necessary to convey the same meaning. On the other hand you can very often tell the importance of an exhibition by noting how many of the exhibitors carry their captions in more than one language.

'Advantages' are important for the sales director, the buyer and the accountant. 'Applications' are particularly useful for the foreman and his team.

Advantages

- Incorporates pre-heater, evaporator, condenser in one casing
- Compact unit
- High evaporation capacity
- High separation efficiencies
- Possibility to control the residence time
- Energy - economy
- Perfect sealing
- Good wetting properties
- Flexible units, suitable for specific requirements of customer
- Self cleaning
- Operational safety, facilitated maintenance
- Can be completely dismantled
- Simple installation

Luwa Pulspak ®

Application

Evaporation and distillation in small and medium size firms in the chemical industry:
- Separation of organic solvents
- Reclamation of solvents
- Concentration of aqueous solutions (also including slurries)
- Distillation of explosive products
- Concentration of plant extracts
- Volume reduction of effluents

Luwa

mounting method, the lighting must all be included. It is important, also, to agree a price before work starts, and to specify to whom the finished piece belongs, especially if it is to be a work of art rather than a straightforward model or feature.

Most specialists are individuals working alone or with only a small group. It is quite accepted practice for them to ask for some initial money to buy the materials they need to start work. The essential thing, of course, is to choose an expert or artist with whom you and, most vitally, your designer, get on. Don't allow the excuse of creativity to override the realism of good business practice, and be prepared to offer backup administrative support.

You will need to control the specialists' deadlines, and to stop them going over the top and producing a result which is far too dominant. There is no easy way of handling this, but you, and more particularly your designer, need to keep a regular eye on progress at the artist's studio. Indeed, this applies to all such specialist creative work. It does need a lot of supervision because the artist is not working to a precisely evolved aim laid out to the last detail in your designer's drawings. He is creating as he goes along.

KINDS OF FEATURE

Scale models

Most professional scale-model makers earn their living by producing architectural and structural models. But many of them are highly skilled, too, at other types such as landscape and product models, and some may specialise in cut-away models. Most model making is done by fair-sized companies with experts working in plastics (particularly acrylic), metals and wood. They also make use of a lot of standard bought-in products such as scale trees, people and vehicles.

As a general rule their work is very precise and highly detailed, but it tends to lack atmosphere and the patina of real life. Despite this, most people love looking at models, and apart from slides or a film, a scale model is often the only way you can show your company's activities. How else can you exhibit a container ship, or the inside of an atomic reactor, or the layout of an automated factory producing doors, from new lumber to final pack?

Dioramas and glass paintings

These are much more theatrical. Their one major exhibition drawback is that they can only be viewed from one side, and they have to be set up like a theatre stage complete with proscenium arch. Because of this they are not often used commercially – perhaps a good reason for using them!

They represent foreground, middle ground, far ground and background on different levels. In a diorama the first two are actually modelled in perspective whilst the far ground and background are painted to take the eye on into the distance. The eye reads a well-made diorama as a single continuous view.

Glass paintings are made on much the same principle of breaking up the view into 'grounds' but in this case the effect is achieved by painting on parallel sheets of glass rather as in a Victorian peepshow. To be effective they have to be viewed from the front, through a restricted proscenium. The diorama technique, however, can be used without a proscenium if it is on a large enough scale and supported by full-size foreground details. This technique has been successfully used by museums round the world. It would be an expensive way of creating a display for a single temporary exhibition, though it might well be trucked from venue to venue as part of a series of exhibitions.

A very effective use of diorama and modelling techniques is 'Pepper's Ghost', originally a phantom produced on the Victorian stage by a sheet of glass reflecting an actor under the stage. It creates the illusion that one view is fading into another before the onlooker's eyes. Relying entirely on lighting and a 45-degree sheet of glass, it can be a good and novel way of getting across 'Before' and 'After' presentations.

Murals and sculptures

Any artistic feature, such as these, will depend completely on the individual style and skill of the artist you choose. You and your designer have an opportunity here to exert useful patronage and encouragement to artists by using their work as an adjunct to exhibit design. Before you finally agree to proceed, you should always ask the artist to produce a sketch or maquette of his proposals for an agreed fee. Any commission should include provision for abandoning the project if unsatisfactory at this stage, otherwise you may subsequently spend a great deal of money to no good purpose. In-

Six simple panels moving from the general to the particular which can be used in a number of other ways after the exhibition, back in the office or out on the road. If there is room, the panels will be better on their own so that you can read them without having to bend down.

'Advantages' and 'benefits' are always popular and are good messages to direct at the visitor.

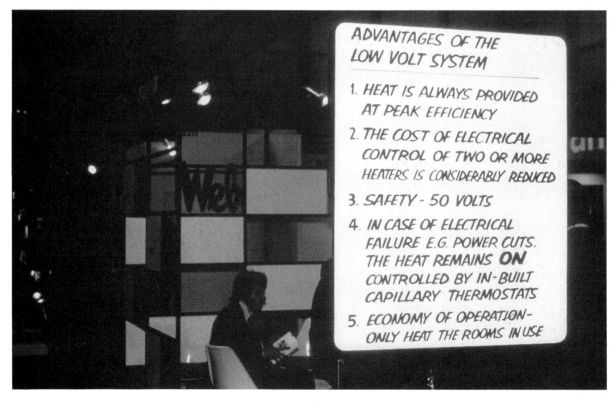

cidentally, don't forget to keep any sketches or models, as they may turn out to be both valuable and decorative if you have picked a good artist who subsequently becomes popular.

Flags, banners and fabrics features

Bunting has long been associated with celebration. Both outside and indoors the primary colours and swags and patterns created form splendidly exotic features. Yet today, apart from very basic use of banners and simple stretched velaria roofs and drape dividers between simple shell schemes, we seem to have forgotten how effective fabrics can be in exhibition work. These few examples show how good even quite simple ideas can be.

Incidentally, fabric is the cheapest way of filling large areas of space, and exhibition organisers themselves should more often practise the art of celebration at their entrances and in casual voids.

Maps showing locations are always popular, but listing addresses and telephone numbers often amounts to a waste of space and an unnecessary cost. This information is usually contained in sales brochures, and your staff are available on the stand to write out the address and telephone number of your nearest office, in any case.

Water features

Any form of water, particularly if it is moving, makes a calming and enjoyable feature, but strictly it should be used only if it relates in some way to your business. A plastic fountain stuck out front is not really appropriate, nor is a watery grotto in the corner unless it is product-related.

Specialist firms will provide almost anything you are likely to need in the way of underwater lighting, pumps, fountains and containers. But be warned that water engineers seem apt to underpower the capacity of their effects, so insist on a demonstration before the display arrives on site. And watch for the problem of containing the water properly; you do not want to flood your display, and your visitors will not appreciate getting soaked.

Most water features will have recirculating systems, so it is important to filter out the cigarette ends. Make sure the supplier maintains the system for you during the show and regularly cleans it out (without making it smell like a public swimming bath). Finally, you must make arrangements for emptying the pool at the end of the exhibition; not many stands are conveniently built over the plug hole.

A useful literature rack which helps visitors choose the information they want. However, only use it for giveaway literature of no great intrinsic value. Expensive literature should only be given in exchange for a name and address.

Giant photographs and holograms

If you pick the right images, giant photographs can be simple and spectacular eyecatchers. Colour is expensive, and black and white can be most effective. You can print your black and white pictures on colour-dyed paper or even bleach out your black and white images and replace them using colour dyes; or you can make sepia prints or colour-tint them. All these techniques will cost about twice the amount of a black and white print, but this is still a lot less than the cost of full colour.

A Japanese company has recently introduced a process, available around the world, which takes a colour transparency and by using a four-colour spray head reproduces the image onto paper, fabric, or even carpet. Working on the principle of a computer scanning the original and instructing the robot spray head, it is being increasingly used to produce television scenery, but is also extremely effective as the backcloth for an exhibit.

Also making use of modern technology are holograms of three-dimensional images of objects, based on laser projection. These are still at an early stage, but they have already been used in commercial exhibition work and hold out great possibilities for the future. They need very carefully controlled light conditions, though, and are still very expensive to produce. Safety regulations also restrict the use of lasers.

Demonstrations

Demonstrations are a sure way to bring in the crowds. You may decide to have a complete four-colour lithographic press producing special exhibition issues at top speed (even the Great Exhibition of 1851 had moving machinery, including the *Illustrated London News*' latest press) or you may settle for a one-off salesman selling a new apple-peeling 'gizmo' exactly as his mediaeval trade fair predecessors used to. Either way, demonstration is a highly effective special feature. Everyone likes to watch experts at work, and you must allow space for your visitors to stand (or sit) and view. It may even be worth building a demonstration theatre, which will also provide a rather less noisy and better-controlled area for the presenter and his demonstration. But it must not block the gangway; the fire/safety office could shut you down if this happens. And it must not cause unnecessary disturbance to your neighbours; if it does, the organisers could stop you demonstrating.

'Hands-on' features

Often second only to demonstrations in popularity are features which invite audience participation. They can prove an exceedingly good gambit to help your sales staff open up communication with an audience. But make sure of two things. You mustn't make the games too long and complicated or all your visitors' time will be spent in playing them. And you must plan how your staff are to introduce themselves and get on with the real business.

A 'hands-on' feature does not mean simply a video show. It can be as simple as a hinged flap, a push button or a 'what the butler saw' zoetrope. Even a 'touch and feel' exhibit, perhaps to show how much better your carpet underlay is than your competitors', can entice the visitor from the gangway onto your stand.

Moiré patterns

These usually take the form of a disc, revolving behind a lightbox face with a graphic diagram on it. This front diagram will probably take the form of a cut-away drawing, of an oil refinery for instance, or the workings of an internal combustion engine. When the patterned disc is revolved behind the front graphic, which also has a regular pattern on it where 'movement' is required, the optical illusion of flowing movement along the diagrammatic pipe occurs, on the visual interframe moiré principle. Specialist companies produce these units to order.

Animated figures

These vary enormously in type and complexity and therefore in price. The overridingly important point is that they must be manufactured by experts. They can vary from simple cartoon figures that have perhaps only one movement to robots that move around your stand. A fairly recent and very effective development involves projecting a film of a face talking onto a simple sculptured face 'screen'. The technique, perhaps that of a well-known entertainer or sportsman or historical figure, creates the illusion that he is permanently there on your stand.

Flowers and planting

An exhibition hall is just about the worst possible environment for live plants. It is hot, dusty, dry and, most importantly, lacking in sunlight. The plants therefore need very carefully controlled conditions designed into their setting and very good regular maintenance by fully trained people. There are

Neatly arranged literature often produces some unusual words. It would be a pity to take any of these leaflets and thus spoil the pattern.

firms which specialise in exhibition planting and you should use one of them. It is no job for amateurs.

The Interior Landscape Group of the British Association of Landscape Industries have produced an excellent guide to the specification of interior landscape which includes a classification of foliage plants into twelve groups. By using this your designer will be able to brief the supplier of the planting. But plants, like people, are individuals. The nursery should always be visited and specific plants chosen. Foliage colour may also be important; these details can only be worked out properly at the nursery.

Planting must be good and solid; there is nothing worse than a plant container which looks as though the vandals have already pulled out the best bits. No soil or compost should be visible unless it is part of the design. Boulders, pebbles and grit can be useful if you have problems like running a bed below an exhibit. The exhibition planting firms will be able to provide you with whatever you need, often including props that can be hired such as urns and other containers, which may be used as part of the design.

You may decide that you want flowering plants such as chrysanthemums to add colour to the display. Again, the specialists will help. Do not forget that quite spectacular effects such as floral clocks and title captions can be produced if called for; these particularly come into their own in exterior agricultural shows.

Even if you use artificial plants and flowers – and these are sometimes very good – they will still need regular maintenance in the form of dusting and cleaning. Cut flower arrangements for the stand have to be done daily, and should be checked during the day if possible. Again it pays to use experts who know what will survive the rigours best. Perhaps you will want to enliven your staff badges with a daily buttonhole; if your firm's name is Pink Rose Kitchens, what better than to have all your staff wear a pink rose? Buttonholes form a useful secondary identification and may persuade the visitor to spend a little longer checking out your representative's name and company position when first introduced. Again, the florist will help with these as with the cut flowers.

DISPLAY WORK

Bringing the product to the fore

One of the main reasons for being at any exhibition is to seize the chance of showing your actual product and not just pictures of it – a job far better done anyway by leaflets, which can also be taken away by potential clients for future reference.

In the 1950s and 1960s the structure of the stand itself had become so dominant that it became quite difficult to find any actual products at all on some stands. But one advantage of the extraordinary increase in construction costs in recent years has been to make exhibitors aware of the way in which structure had been taking over at the expense of content.

A result of this dominance was that in the process much of the expertise of exhibition techniques was ignored or lost. We need now to restore this expertise and to put the product itself out front again.

Creating the display with the product

Don't be afraid to use shop window methods to create the display. Many of the techniques of exhibition display started life as window display design in large stores, one of the first places where artists were employed to help sell goods.

Using the product is an obvious way of creating the display. In the past, exhibitors sometimes managed to give the impression that the whole stand was built from their product, so that the visitor had no excuse for not knowing what was being sold. Some of the Victorian exhibition trophies were quite over the top, but it is the unlikely feature that may work best. The one thing that is remembered about the gigantic 1924 British Empire Exhibition at Wembley is the refrigerated display sculpture, life-size, of the Prince of Wales (later Edward VIII), moulded in Australian butter. We don't know HRH's own view of this exhibit, or whose the copyright was; but we do remember Australian butter.

SOME EXAMPLES OF DISPLAY

Some products are just too big or too dangerous to show in public. This is where the model maker can come to your rescue, with models of the oil rig you have just completed or cut-away diagrammatic models of the centre of the nuclear reactor you are currently building. But much more ordinary products can create display problems too.

Carpets, for instance, are rarely well shown. Often, they end up even being displayed on walls. But when you are buying a carpet there is only one logical place to view it, and that is on the floor. So ways have to be found of displaying carpets at that level. Perhaps you can build some variable height plinths with the carpet samples on top and let your visitors walk across a ramped route looking down on them. The ramp itself can be carpeted with various carpet sections, and the side rails of the ramp can contain details of the product. Add some suitable spaces along the route for the sales staff and your stand will then do the sales job well and be more helpful to the visitor at the same time.

Similarly, rolls of material always seem to end up in untidy heaps or, at best, standing on their ends. But try unrolling them and doing gigantic 'ribbon' displays. And look too in the large department stores to see how they are displaying their fabrics. You will often find an idea you can use on your stand, even if your product is not soft furnishing.

Perhaps the worst displayed products are raw materials. Just how can you display things like timber, aggregates, coal, stone, wheat, corn? The answer is, as with most display techniques, in a hundred and one ways, so long as nobody panics. Otherwise you will end up with boxes full of kinds of sand or, worse, samples on laboratory sample dishes.

Raw materials were something which most Victorian exhibitions had masses of; so what did they do? They mostly used them decoratively: big high glass jars with different aggregates or sands arranged in colourful layers; sections of actual trees built in exotic structures; coal sculpted into replicas of classical statuary; stone built into exotic grottoes – perhaps not ideal solutions to today's display needs, but with a little up-dating much better solutions than most. And they all had one major thing in their favour – they were made almost entirely from the product.

Very simple (but very effective) features can be created using the product itself. Perhaps you produce tinned Italian-style spaghetti – why not a leaning tower of Pisa built out of your tins? Or do you produce a range of tinned goods? If so, try arranging a 'wall' of tins so that the different coloured labels form a pattern which includes your trade name. In the right context oversized models of your products can be effective too. Though the possibilities are endless, how often do we actually see the product at the forefront of the display, particularly in medium-size exhibitions? All it needs is some creative thought, and if there is a bit of humour in it as well, so much the better.

EXHIBIT MOUNTING

There is only one golden rule for exhibit mounting. If at all possible it should be invisible to the visitors. Among the standard tools and materials used for achieving this are double-sided adhesive pads and tapes, specially built clear acrylic supports, clear nylon filament, a staple-tacking gun, special dressmaker's pin inserters and dressmaker's light-weight pin hammers.

SECURITY

In mounting exhibits you have, unhappily, to be aware that there may be thieves about who will not be stopped by a length of nylon thread.

If you have costly items on your stand there are precautions you must take. Every item should be security-marked and recorded so that, should it

Visitors should never be expected to bend down in order to pick up literature from the floor or to read captions which are not at a convenient height.

If you put a weight on top of your literature, people are unlikely to take it. This may be all right if you want to give it away in exchange for a name and address. No matter how good visitors' eyesight, too, the bottom lines here are going to be very difficult to read unless they get on their hands and knees.

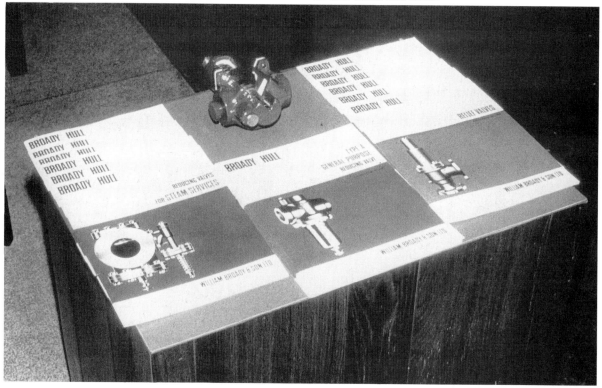

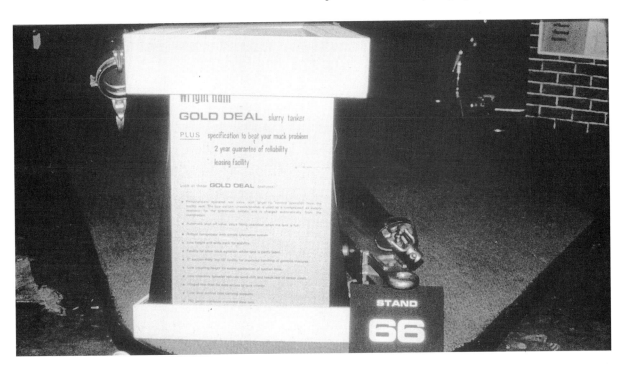

As you can see from the size of the visitor looking at the stand, the information and the leaflet are only likely to attract small children who may be fine in a supermarket but are not going to be much help at an exhibition.

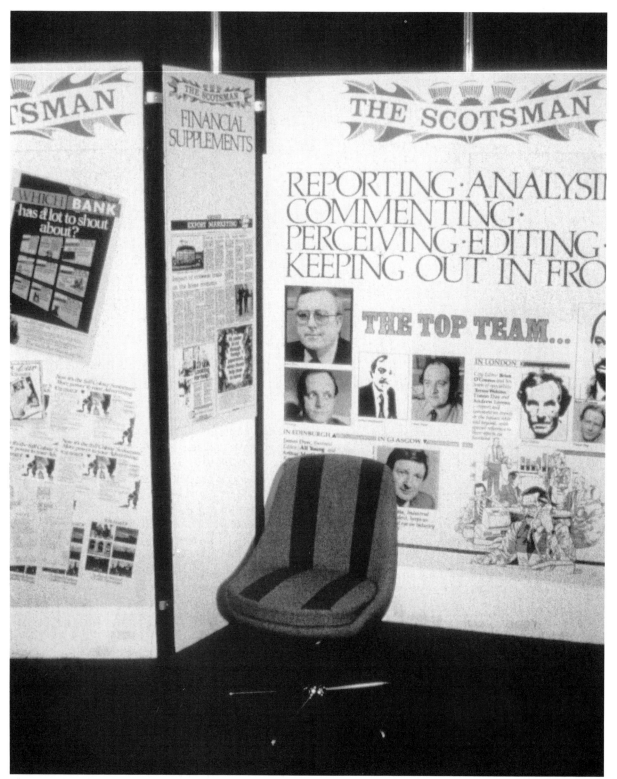

It's nice to fill all the white space on a stand but if you then put a chair in the way, visitors may miss the most interesting part of the message. In this case it is not even necessary to use the space lower down because there is plenty of room on the top of the stand to place freestanding notices.

Having attracted visitors onto your stand and got into conversation, you may be missing a lot of other people. If you intend to have detailed discussing on your stand, make sure there are enough staff also to deal with casual questions from passers-by.

disappear, the police can identify it as your property if they are lucky enough to retrieve it. Your local police anti-crime unit will be able to advise you about the various marking methods, such as engraving and the use of hidden marks, which show up only under ultra-violet light.

As for securing exhibits or fitting alarms to them, the options range from chaining or wiring them down onto the stand structure, to pressure pads which will operate if anyone lifts the exhibit. Expert security firms will be able to advise you and show you the full range of alternatives; and your designer probably has experience of security problems as well.

Some exhibits may have other kinds of problem in terms of conservation. You may need refrigerated cabinets for your displays, and these can be hired if you have food products which need to be kept cold or which need to be kept safe because they are fragile. But don't forget to have the cabinet connected to a separate circuit so that it is not turned off at night with your stand lights.

Or you may be displaying jewellery or silver which could easily go black if the display cases are lined with the wrong kind of display fabric. Your designer should seek the advice of the local museum conservation department if necessary.

Display cases for precious jewels will need to be glazed with bandit or bullet-proof glass and fitted with special locks. Your insurance company will almost certainly specify what you must do, but you may be wise to do rather more than meet their minimum requirements.

Hiring security guards

If you have special high risk items or very valuable products, you may prefer to hire a security guard to stay on your stand overnight. Make sure that you have agreed this beforehand with the organisers and that the exhibition night security team are also in touch. There are both advantages and disadvantages in using the organisers' own security team, but the most effective solution (and the one which will let you sleep at night) is to use your own company security staff.

Remember that buildup and breakdown times are fraught with security problems. At some exhibition halls it may be possible to deposit expensive items in a strong room or large safe. Depending on the product, you may also need security cameras or daytime security guards in obvious attendance as well.

Epilogue

The key figure in almost everything that has gone before is the Exhibit Manager. He is the galvaniser who must make it all happen, the pivot round whom it must all revolve. So this epilogue is addressed to him.

Reading is easy: you start at the beginning and go through to the end. But as well as reading, you have to mark, learn and inwardly digest. As you do so you will rapidly realise how true the first paragraph of this epilogue is, and realise too that the reality on the ground is sometimes sadly unrelated to the logical pattern of the text.

Of course you may be lucky enough to work in an impeccably efficient organisation. But the chances are that your company will be some way into participating in the exhibition before you are actually given the job of Exhibit Manager. You may be pitched in without any job description (for all the world as though a task of this importance and complexity didn't need one), and you – and others –

may be far from clear about the extent of your authority.

As soon as you have finished your first preliminary reading through of the book, you must set about establishing four essential prerequisites.

You must have, and you must be seen to have, full authority for:

1 the direction of support staff

2 the fixing of meetings, and insisting that everyone needed does in fact come

3 the ordering of resources

4 the control of the budget.

Without this authority the chances of success are slim indeed. With it, and with this book at your elbow, you will be instrumental in unlocking a highly rewarding door for your company. Your job will be exhilarating, exhausting, sometimes alarming – and in the end wonderfully satisfying. Go to it!

Sixty Step Checklist

1 *The decision to exhibit*
Before deciding to exhibit, agree your objectives. Identify your target audience groups. Are you out to develop a market, to infiltrate one or to explore one? These objectives must be clear to everyone concerned before you proceed.

2 *Reserve your site*
Agree size and location of site with the organisers. Relate this to your overall budget. Make sure site is right for your produce, e.g. exhibiting PVC drainpipes in a Plastics section would be wasteful if you later found that there was a separate section devoted to drainage.

3 *Agree budget*
Expenditure has four main headings:

(a) Direct expenses
(b) Exhibit material expenses
(c) Visitor promotion expenses
(d) Staff expenses

The Exhibit Manager, who controls the budget, should draw up a progress chart working back from opening day. All key stages should be deadlined, all joint meeting dates established, and each participant must then work to his own date schedule.

4 *Appoint stand designer*
The designer must be carefully briefed, fully understand the nature and structure of your organisation and know to whom he is directly responsible. The Exhibit Manager must check the quality of the work of specialist designers under consideration, and their ability to keep within budget and deliver on time. Resist simply handing the design problem to your top draughtsman or even your talented architectural student son.

5 *Agree product display*
Decide exactly the range and quantity of the products you intend to display. Remember to incorporate any ancillary equipment or machinery needed to display your product to maximum effect; demonstrations attract visitors, gain attention and often get press photographs.

6 *Order and prepare special exhibits*
If you are using a basic shell stand supplied by the organisers, you may have to design only an interior display. With independent stands, sizes and weights of all components must be passed to designer and contractor as soon as possible.

Specially made components and machines must be delivered on site well in advance. If not, there may not be time to set up exhibits properly, and your moving miracle may remain stationary for lack of pre-opening testing time.

7 *Arrange transport*
Bulky products may need special transport, and you should check the route from cargo door to stand. Order transport in good time, not forgetting the return journey. If you need a crane or a fork lift truck check that drivers belong to the appropriate unions.

6 *Brief the designer*
The fullest brief is essential. It must include weights and dimensions, fire and safety regulations, and the organisers' rules and regulations, since these may restrict plans to use special materials. Always discuss likely problems with designer and organisers before taking final decisions.

9 *Stand design*
Shell schemes are intended to save you money; don't duplicate the facilities they offer. Your designer must be familiar with the industry you are selling to, and his design must focus on the product, not distract attention from it.

10 *Order special services*
Demonstrating your product may call for special electrical, water, compressed air and other services. Water needs drainage; compressed air may have to be supplied in bottles; if extra high voltage is needed it must be specified. Remember machines in motion have stronger appeal than static exhibits, but you must comply with Health and Safety at Work requirements.

11 *Arrange stand cleaning*
Grubby finger marks and dust don't enhance your products. Organisers usually attend to gangways, but you will need daily stand cleaners.

12 *Order plumbing fitments*
If you have water and waste disposal make sure it won't cause a flood, and that you can turn off the supply without dismantling the stand. If you are using a tank or pool you will have to empty it on closing day.

13 *Order extras such as furniture, flowers and phones*
Organisers often provide these at bulk discount rates.

Phones are hired from British Telecom or, in the US, the national or regional equivalent service. Get your number from them early on so that you can tell your office and contacts. And make sure the phone is locked away at night; illicit calls to Canadian cousins are expensive.

14 *Arrange insurance*
Discuss with your insurance brokers. Make sure that existing third party insurance for your own exhibits and staff also covers liability to organisers and to all visitors. There are hazards in exhibitions which may not be covered by your existing policy, and the organisers' rules may pass further requirements on to you. With costly stands you should take out contingency cover against cancellation, postponement or shortening of the exhibition. Almost certainly any additional insurance will be cheaper if added to insurances you already have.

15 *Supply name board details*
Display the name by which your company or group is known. Initials are fine if they are in familiar use, but omit Co, Ltd, or plc. Trade names for sign boards are not recommended. Visitors need to identify your stand by familiar name or symbol, and the nameboard must be visible to them as they walk along the gangway as well as when they turn to face your stand.

16 *Approve stand design*
There is no need for an extravagant stand, which will hardly be seen when it is surrounded by crowds. Simple good design is best, preferably incorporating a moving feature to catch the eye. Remember that for most people your stand is your identity, the only visual record of your company for most of your existing clients as well as for newcomers.

17 *Submit plans to organisers*
The stand must conform to national and local planning requirements, and to the rules and regulations of hall owners and organisers. The organisers may need to see your plans, though not necessarily, if you use their shell scheme.

18 *Tender to stand contractor*
If you nominate a stand contractor who has worked before with you or your designer you are virtually obliged to accept his price. If you go out to tender, make sure the plans are fully approved. Stick to the designer's specifications; last minute alterations escalate costs.

19 *Appoint and brief stand contractor*
Choose the best tender from the quotations received. The Exhibit Manager must work with your designer and executive staff to resolve areas of on-site responsibility during the build-up period. Who will be responsible, for instance, for delivery of the major exhibits, and for their packing and return afterwards?

20 *Approve working details*
Make sure your contractor knows which items he has to collect and which will be delivered. Note delivery dates of print items, photographs and special services if they form part of the stand design.

21 *Stand building or prefabrication*
This is the contractor's responsibility, but keep a check on him. Typographical errors often creep in, only to be spotted too late; avoid the same kind of thing happening with your stand. Try to visualise it as it will appear on the big day. Test machines both before they leave the works and after installation; and make sure they are fully provided with safety guards. Keep costs down by prefabricating as much of your stand as possible in the contractor's workshops.

22 *Plan staff requirements*
Manning a stand is not a staff perk and must not

turn into a staff party. Decide how many people you need at any one time and recruit only your best sales and technical staff. Maintain enough demonstrators for your products at all times, and plan for peak periods. Organise rest periods. Try to keep the same staff on the stand throughout, so that they act as a team and improve with each day's experience. After all, in football only two substitutes are allowed.

23 *Select staff*
Give them ample warning. Their business lives may need re-arranging; certainly their private lives will. Holidays may be at stake and your key salesman may be planning a honeymoon or a house-moving.

24 *Staff training programme*
Experience shows that exhibitors spend more time on the first day answering staff queries than the enquiries of visitors. Teach staff as a team and they will act as one. Better still, show them a training film such as 'How not to exhibit yourself'. Tell them the company's objective in exhibiting; tell them about the exhibition and the various facets of the industry it caters for; tell them how to deal with 'market researchers' and with staff from your competitors.

25 *Arrange staff roster*
Short duty periods with breaks are best; two hours with a twenty-minute break is quite long enough. Make sure that staff know the hall layout, the rest periods agreed and how to take a break right away from the stand. Plan for peak times; understaffing is only possible when the pressure is off. The organisers should have detailed figures on hourly attendance flows.

26 *Invite overseas agents*
Ample notice, perhaps several months, of your intention to exhibit is essential to overseas agents. Don't forget to invite other export contacts too. Keep every useful contact posted about any new developments being introduced at this exhibition.

27 *Arrange hotel accommodation*
Book well in advance, for your own staff as well as your overseas agents; every other exhibitor will have the same priorities. Staff accommodation should be cosy rather than costly, and handy for the exhibition centre, not miles out of town.

28 *Prepare visitor lists*
Time spent drawing up a list of prospects by name can pay dividends later. Look to new prospects for new business and to known contacts for more business. Phone your main prospects to ask what day and what time they will be visiting your stand.

29 *Order tickets and badges*
Fill in the organisers' forms for these in good time. Delays or failure to deliver could lead to your staff wasting valuable time on opening day, or having to pay to get in.

30 *Prepare ticket despatch*
Your representatives can be used to distribute invitation tickets personally; but whatever method you use, don't issue them so early that they get lost, or so late that busy prospects have no time to make arrangements to visit the exhibition.

31 *Despatch tickets overseas*
Your overseas contacts may want to plan an extended business trip taking in your exhibition *en route*. In any event, give them ample notice.

32 *Despatch tickets in United Kingdom*
Consider whether to include also a letter or a catalogue, perhaps an invitation to a reception. Decide what you can afford and what is most likely to attract your important visitor.

33 *Plan advertising and publicity policy*
Call in your advertising, publicity and promotion experts to formulate a co-ordinated plan using all the media at your disposal to add marketing muscle. Try also to tie in with any plans the organiser may have.

34 *Agree backup advertising*
Your normal advertisements in trade and technical press should mention your participation in the exhibition, its date and venue. Make sure you include your stand number and ask the organiser if there is a special exhibition symbol you can use.

35 *Place backup advertising overseas*
Overseas advertising may help a local sales drive. Discuss in good time with your agent, as he may want valuable customers to see the exhibition and to consider co-ordinating a visit.

36 *Place backup advertising in United Kingdom*
The exhibition may call for extra advertising beyond your routine schedule. Check if the organisers are offering other opportunities besides the catalogue. Posters at the exhibition site or hall could help direct visitors to your stand.

37 *Despatch copy overseas*
Advertisements carrying client-approved trans-
lated copy should be sent in camera copy form
wherever possible. Send a copy to overseas agents as
they may be able to use their influence to get it
properly placed in local publications. Send any
supporting press releases and photographs to the
editors at the same time.

38 *Despatch copy in United Kingdom*
Book your advertising space in good time. A really
well-prepared press release for trade and technical
press could give an added boost to your product
before, during or after the exhibition.

39 *Photographs*
You will want photographs for advertising, publicity, sales leaflets and literature, and all entail
separate briefing of the photographer. Copies
should be available in the organisers' press office for
visiting journalists. You should also have record
photographs of your finished stand. Use only official
photographers and be selective in your choice of
prints; buy on approval and don't order more shots
than you need.

40 *Place advertisement in exhibition catalogue*
This is perhaps your best advertising medium. The
catalogue acts as a reference book long after the
exhibition is over. List your company name,
address, phone number, and telex or cable address.
Text should identify the products exhibited so that
buyers and specifiers using the catalogue as a
buyer's guide can get in touch with you later.

41 *Trade literature on stand*
It is wise to categorise your trade literature, with
well-produced but inexpensive give-away material
for the casual visitor and selective distribution of
more costly brochures for genuinely interested
visitors who give their names and addresses.
Maintain good stocks of everything.

42 *Arrange translations*
Wherever possible, have these checked in the
respective countries beforehand. This may take a
little longer but it is essential if you want to be
considered a serious exporter.

43 *Typesetting*
Draw up a schedule with your print designer and
printer. Overnight typesetting charges to meet a last
minute panic can be exorbitant.

44 *Print delivery*
Make sure that printed material is delivered at least
a month before opening day. Advance copies should
go to leading customers, and stand staff will need to
memorise the contents. Do not have literature
delivered direct to the exhibition site by printers; it
is often mislaid and is a cause of unnecessary panic.

45 *Complete advertising literature plans*
Make a final check that all advertising has been
properly placed and that the various publications
are sending voucher copies. Have up-to-date price
lists and names and addresses of agents available on
stand for opening day.

46 *Prepare press release Number One*
Prepared months before, this general release,
announcing your company's presence at the
exhibition and briefly detailing any new products to
be shown, should have a wide circulation.

47 *Prepare press release Number Two*
This is aimed at the trade and technical press. It will
feature more details of products and should contain
photographs or illustrations, including a picture of
your stand, and perhaps an artist's impression or a
photograph of the model.

48 *Prepare press release Number Three*
This is aimed at catching the interest of your local
press.

49 *Prepare press release Number Four*
This could include a bumper issue of your house
journal, which might feature a story on the growth
of your company and other background information.

50 *Arrange press reception*
The organisers' responsibility is to publicise the
exhibition as a whole, not individual exhibitors or
products. Consider holding your own reception on
your stand or in a nearby private room. Make sure it
does not clash with your competitors' receptions
and time it to catch the journalists' deadline.

51 *Send out invitations to the reception*
Make phone calls a week before the opening to remind guests who have not replied to your invitation to come along. Decide who among your executives is to make the welcoming speech and answer press questions.

52 *Final organisation of press reception*
Have press kits of background information, copies of speeches, and photographs available. Make sure the caterer knows when to start and when to stop.

53 *Arrange photographer*
Although you are hosting the press, you may want your own record of important visitors to your stand or your reception for use in other publications, including your own house journal.

54 *Prepare continuing and final press releases*
Pictures and reports of your visitors could be used in the trade press through your own contacts or in your local press at home. The number of enquiries you received or the value of business done during the exhibition would also make good follow-up stories.

55 *Check stand on eve of opening*
If everything has been properly planned, the final check should show it all dovetailing into place. It is too late now to make alterations.

56 *Hold buyers' receptions*
Arrange these for opening day and/or for subsequent days as necessary.

57 *Maintain your stand*
You must maintain your stand throughout and ensure that all materials are provided, including supplies of literature, and that working models and slide shows are working all the time.

58 *Monitor each day's achievements*
Your planned objectives should be reached daily. There are bound to be surprises; you may need extra technical staff. Hold debriefing meeting at end of day one. How did you cope? How many names and addresses of new prospects did you take? How many sales?

59 *Dismantle stand*
When the exhibition is over, the temptation will be to get away fast. Resist it; there is much to be done. Transport and removal of exhibits must be organised and carried through. Your overseas agents may want to use your display material, so make sure it is carefully dismantled and packed away.

60 *Conduct post-mortem*
Back in the office, compile your overall report. Was it all worth the effort? Check invoices. And don't forget to reserve your site for next year's show.

Part Three

ESSENTIAL INFORMATION

In this section you will find specimen letters, explanatory drawings, examples of exhibition design practice, checklists, standard forms and other useful material. Much of it is referred to in the foregoing text and we hope that the rest is self-explanatory. The material comes from many different sources and in many cases has been edited and revised for this book.

COST ESTIMATING BUDGET

Introduction

The Exhibitor's Planning Guide below has been devised to help all who participate in exhibitions. The project manager for each exhibition should find this guide useful in helping to identify the likely costs when arranging his company's stand. The Guide attempts to cover all aspects of exhibition participation and appears long and detailed but many of the headings are optional and others would not be appropriate in every case. Sometimes the various headings and sub-headings will act as a reminder rather than identify an exceptional cost.

Prepared by _____

Date_____

Update _____

Main Headings	Subsidiary Headings	Code	Budget	Actual	Notes	
1.00 Direct Expenses	1.01 **Space cost** 1.02 **Shell scheme** 1.03 **Stand Fitting** Display Typographer/ Graphics Model 1.04 **Additional services** Electricity & Gas Water & Waste Compressed air Refrigeration Telephone Flowers Tickets 1.05 **Insurance** 1.06 **Cleaning** 1.07 **Furniture & Carpet hire** 1.08 **Professional fees** Designer Architect Engineer 1.09 **Management visits** 1.10 **Contingency**				1.01 1.02 1.03 1.04 1.05 1.06 1.08 1.09 1.10	Note payment dates. If compulsory, ensure no double costs at 1.03. Quote in good time, appoint early, then work to reduce final costs. See if consumption included with connections or separate. Take meter readings before and at close. Add to your existing company policy and consider separate contingency insurance for abandonment or curtailment, and third party risk. Often included. If not, see what is. Money spent here should increase effectiveness and remove worry. Go and see, talk, prepare and reduce surprises (always expensive). Calculate 15% for the total of the items here which are not already contractually organised.
2.00 Exhibit Material	2.01 **In-house** 2.02 **Bought-in** 2.03 **Assembly** 2.04 **Storage** 2.05 **Testing** 2.06 **Transportation** 2.07 **Lifting** 2.08 **Contingency**				2.01 2.02 2.03/5 2.06/7 2.08	Tell them early, coordinate lifting and transport and make sure fixings relate. Stick to standard sizes and avoid specials. Don't allow pc items when tendering to permit late escalations. It takes time – can you do this at the works and avoid storage? Remember, both to and from the exhibition. If you have done your budgeting accurately only 10% should be necessary for contingency.

Main Headings	Subsidiary Headings	Code	Budget	Actual	Notes	

3.00 Visitor Promotion	3.01 Advertising
	  Press
	  Radio
	  TV
	  Posters
	  Point of sale
	  Direct mail
	3.02 Catalogue/Buyers Guide
	  Advertisements
	  Extra copies
	  Extra indices
	3.03 Technical press advertising
	3.04 Technical Literature
	  Design
	  Translations
	  Blocks
	  Printing
	3.05 P.R. staff fees & expenses
	3.06 Entertaining
	3.07 Receptions
	3.08 Press Releases
	3.09 Press photographer
	3.10 VIP visits
	3.11 Special visits
	3.12 Contingency
					3.01
					
					3.02
					
					3.03
					
					3.04
					
					3.05
					3.08
					
					3.10
					
					3.11
					3.12
						Supplement organisers own promotion and pinpoint your company in particular.
						Remember buyers guide for future use.
						Tell your Ad. Agent and incorporate your participation in all your ads for months before. Take ads in industry supplements?
						How much of what quality in which languages for which audience categories? Avoid expensive late reprints.
						Co-ordinate with organisers.
						Appoint someone on stand to deal with all press and photographers.
						Liaise with organisers and bring your own, including head office and foreign buyers.
						Prizes, competitions.
						Probably sensible to allow 20% on your contingency so that you can take advantage of good ideas arriving later.

4.00 Staff Costs	4.01 Temporary Staff Costs Demonstrators 4.02 Training 4.03 Films 4.04 Courses 4.05 Briefing 4.06 Hotel 4.07 Travel & Car Parking 4.08 Subsistence 4.09 Security 4.10 Staff uniforms 4.11 Badges & passes 4.12 Interpreters 4.13 Contingency				4.02 4.03 4.05 4.06 4.09 4.10/11 4.12 4.13	Reps and salesmen need training to take advantage of exhibition differences See Video Arts 2 films 'OK on the day' and 'How not to Exhibit yourself'. Don't leave it to opening day – you will miss valuable visitors. Book in time – it's for rest and relaxation, not living it up. Personal as well as product. Personnel identification can be casual and effective to help visitors. What foreign audience are you attracting? These costs should be known well in advance and you can probably confine your contingency sum to 5%.
5.00 Overseas Exhibitions (Extra Expenses)	5.01 Freight & Shipping 5.02 Forwarding & Transport 5.03 Bond 5.04 Customs Clearing 5.05 Insurance 5.06 Re-packing at Conclusion 5.07 Temporary Storage 5.08 Return Transport Charges 5.09 Return Shipping Charges 5.10 Contingency				5.03 5.04 5.05 5.06 5.07 5.10	Some countries will require goods to be bonded. Depending on country, various charges for clearance can be made. Various goods require specific insurance. If goods are not to be left, re-packing and shipping will be necessary. Could involve temporary storage if staying overseas. Advisable to allow a small contingency – say 5% to 10%.

Source: 'Costing out the Exhibition', Andry Montgomery Ltd, July 1987

ORGANISATIONAL SCHEDULE/CHECKLIST OF ACTIVITIES IN ORGANISING AN EXHIBIT

1 Decide to exhibit
2 Reserve site
3 Agree budget
4 Appoint stand designer
5 Agree product display
6 Order and prepare special exhibits
7 Arrange transport
8 Brief stand designer (check rules & regulations)
9 Stand design
10 Order electricity, water supply and compressed air
11 Arrange stand cleaning
12 Order plumbing fitments
13 Order stand optional extras, furniture, flowers, etc.
14 Arrange insurance
15 Supply nameboard details
16 Approve stand design
17 Submit plans to organisers
18 Tender to stand contractor
19 Appoint and brief stand contractor
20 Approve working details
21 Stand building (prefabrication)
22 Plan staff requirements
23 Select staff
24 Staff training programme
25 Brief staff
26 Arrange staff roster
27 Invite overseas agents
28 Arrange hotel accommodation
29 Prepare guest lists
30 Order tickets and badges
31 Prepare ticket despatch
32 Despatch tickets overseas
33 Despatch tickets in UK
34 Plan advertising and publicity policy
35 Agree back-up advertising
36 Place back-up advertising overseas
37 Place back-up advertising in UK
38 Despatch copy overseas
39 Despatch copy in UK
40 Photographs
41 Place exhibition advert in exhibition catalogue
42 Stand literature, exhibition technical brochures
43 Arrange translations
44 Typesetting
45 Print delivery
46 Complete advertising/literature plans
47 Prepare press release No. 1
48 Prepare press release No. 2
49 Prepare press release No. 3
50 Prepare press release No. 4
51 Arrange press reception
52 Send out invitations
53 Final organisation of press reception
54 Arrange photographer
55 Arrange continuing press releases
56 Construct stand – exhibition eve
57 Hold receptions
58 The exhibition
59 Dismantle stand
60 Conduct post-mortem

Source: 'What Every Exhibitor Ought to Know', 1976 Interbuild Exhibitions Ltd/Video Arts Ltd.

INSURANCE CHECKLIST

Most exhibition organisers follow a standard format for insurance obligations. The salient requirements are that:

1 Exhibitors insure against all risks, fire, theft etc. the exhibition stand, furnishings, display material and their own products. They also should insure their own staff and visitors against 'public liability'. The period of insurance commences upon entry of standfitting into the venue and ends when the hall has been cleared of all materials.

2 Exhibitors should insure against abandonment or partial closing of the exhibition.

3 For overseas exhibitions goods should be insured in transit. When frozen goods or any perishable products are shipped, 'special peril' insurance may be necessary.

4 Staff on overseas duty should have medical insurance.

Source: AML Rules and Regulations, edited by Alan Taylor

EXHIBITION ENQUIRY FORM

Visitors to stands should have their enquiry recorded for appropriate action to be taken.

An example of a form used for a typical exhibition enquiry is shown below. It is similar to the vouchers used by Visa, American Express, etc.

These forms are often in a three-part set, enabling copies to be sent to appropriate departments such as Publicity or the Sales Office, with final copy to the representative for the visitors' area.

(a) They can be used with a machine when visitors already have an exhibition enquiry plastic card

(b) A visitor's card can be stapled to the form

(c) They can be completed by hand – preferably in block capitals

These should be 'followed up' daily, numbered and recorded in sales records and filed by the appropriate department at head office.

Source: Exhibition Enquiry System, AML

Exhibition Enquiry

Details of Sales Lead

Position in Company

Type of Business

Enquiry Taken by

Date

Telephone

Visitors current project/job

Checklist of action required

☐ Literature given   ☐ Mail literature   ☐ Submit estimate

Date Actioned

STAND MANAGERS' CHECKLIST

1.0 Basic list for management

1.01 Agree objectives

1.02 Establish command

1.03 Establish responsibilities

1.04 Plan all dates backwards from opening day

1.05 Establish a planning calendar

1.06 Fix key meetings well in advance

1.07 Circulate information to all concerned

1.08 Chase progress relentlessly

1.09 Check budgets regularly

1.10 Resist afterthoughts

2.0 Overnight lists – end of preview day and every exhibition day

2.01 Have stand personnel done their homework? Does everyone know:
   (a) Why your company is exhibiting?
   (b) What is featured on the stand?
   (c) What specialist staff will be on the stand?
   (d) The geography of the stand?
   (e) The geography of the venue?
   (f) How to close a stand interview?
   (g) How to record an enquiry?

2.02 Was the stand always tidy and welcoming?

2.03 Has tomorrow's VIP/press visit list been examined and management/staff briefed on background/duties?

2.04 Were catering arrangements working as planned?

2.05 Have visitor enquiries been processed on a day-to-day basis?

3.0 Last exhibiting day

3.01 Are dismantling instructions complete and understood by all concerned?

Source: Various instructions and guidelines collated by Alan Taylor, July 1987

PUBLIC RELATIONS AND PRESS CHECKLIST

Success in an exhibition is directly related to the press coverage and publicity achieved. To maximise this, ensure that:

1 You use all media and promotional opportunities offered, i.e., radio, TV, national, local and trade press, direct mail, exhibition catalogue, receptions, exhibition press office facilities, invitation tickets, poster display, car and lorry stickers, give-aways (if appropriate), personality visits, organisers' visitor promotion 'aids'.

2 Link all advertising to your exhibition stand.

3 Contact all appropriate editors, journalists, radio and TV producers.

4 Ensure overseas officers and representatives receive appropriate PR releases and other publicity aids.

5 Issue press releases regularly.

6 Ensure that press cuttings are regularly collected and filed.

7 Ensure that radio or TV stories are taped or videoed

8 Ensure that monitoring is maintained for at least three months after close of exhibition.

Source: Alan Taylor

SPECIALIST CHECKLIST FOR OVERSEAS SHOWS

Exhibiting overseas is very similar to exhibiting in the UK, with certain exceptions. This checklist highlights particular areas which are different.

Project

1 Inform Export Department and/or local representatives/agents.

2 Call for quotations from freight and shipping forwarders.

3 Apply for any special permits.

4 Arrange all print matters in appropriate languages.

5 Arrange export insurance.

6 Arrange for interpreter – if necessary.

7 Warn Works Department of shipping dates.

8 Keep local agents advised of programme.

Personnel

1 Notify staff of dates they are required overseas.

2 Check staff vaccination/inoculation requirements, if necessary.

3 Check visa requirements.

4 Arrange medical and/or special risk insurance.

5 Obtain '*Hints to Businessmen Overseas*' booklet from BOTB

6 Book air passages (take advantage of special offers or Apex bookings).

7 Book hotel accommodation in good time.

8 Arrange travellers' cheques, currency and staff subsistence.

9 Brief stand manager on meetings with British consul and commercial attaché.

10 Brief staff on local conditions.

11 Brief staff on dismantling and cleaning operation.

12 If long and difficult exhibition – authorise rest and relaxation before return to UK.

13 Brief staff on any local differences in exhibition rules and regulations which may prevail in certain countries.

Source: Alan Taylor

EVALUATION/SURVEY CHECKLIST

Measuring the success of participating in an exhibition is difficult, but it is easy and useful to measure 'relative' success.

The indicator to use is whether visitors are 'useful' or 'not useful'.

Measurement techniques can be used thus:

1 Desirable event
(a) Visitor passing stand and obtaining passing exposure of products.
(b) Visitor walking onto the stand.
(c) Visitor taking literature from stand.
(d) Visitor taking a sample.
(e) Visitor talking to member of stand staff.
(f) A sale being made.
(g) An agent being appointed.
(h) The name of a further contact being obtained.

2 Significant relative success
This method records visitors' reactions on the stand. It requires stand staff to record information on a standard form, providing an evaluation of success. The form illustrated is a method used by Glynwed Limited and developed by Exhibition Audience Audits Ltd, to whom acknowledgement is made. The obligation to complete it tends to concentrate the minds of exhibition stand staff on essentials.

Source: Piers Nicholson, Exhibition Audience Audits Limited, Glynwed Limited

```
              GLYNWED LTD.-INTERNATIONAL BUILDING EXHIBITION
                              "Vogue baths"
```

Your name: *Tony Seward*	**3rd** day	**6** November	Time: **10.30 a.m.**

Fill in the line above NOW.
Then put THREE ticks in one vertical column below for each visitor to the stand with whom you have a conversation, however short.
(For definitions, see back cover.)

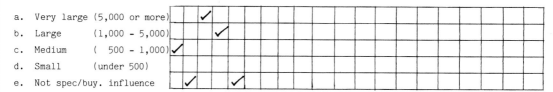

1. VISITOR TYPE   1 2 3 4 5 6 7 8 9 10 11 12 13 14 15 16 17 18 19 20
a. Specifier
b. Buying influence
c. Other visitor

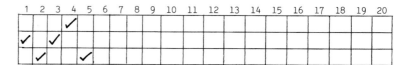

2. IMPORTANCE (baths per year)
a. Very large (5,000 or more)
b. Large   (1,000 - 5,000)
c. Medium   (500 - 1,000)
d. Small   (under 500)
e. Not spec/buy. influence

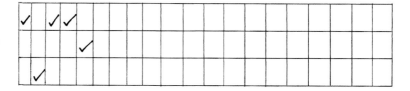

3. PREVIOUS KNOWLEDGE
a. Of at least 1 of our
   products in detail
b. Of our product line in
   general terms
c. No previous knowledge
   of our products

USING THE SERVICES OF ARCHITECTS AND DESIGNERS

RIBA Clients' Advisory Service

The normal services of the architect to the construction industry are generally understood but the architect's design contributions in other fields are less well-known. Many of the imaginative stands at exhibitions demonstrate the architect's flair for understanding and transmitting the exhibitor's message. The same inspiration is evident in the museums that grace many of our cities and inform their people.

Simple, direct terms and 'Plain English' technical literature are far the most palatable and understandable. Many architects create such literature and illustrate it in a way that supports its persuasive character. Nothing is more expensive than technical literature that is ill-understood.

The Clients' Advisory Service of the Royal Institute of British Architects gives clients the opportunity to look at the records of architects in their many fields of activity, and the service is free. Informed choice is available through this service to all clients, whatever their problem.

Clients' Advisory Service, RIBA, 66 Portland Place, London WIN 4AD (Tel: 01-580 5533).

Chartered Society of Designers: Designers' Register

The Designers' Register at the Chartered Society of Designers (formerly the Society of Industrial Artists and Designers) provides rapid access to full information on design practices and freelance designers, all of whom are Chartered Society of Designers members. Individual client requirements are carefully matched with the skills, experience and expertise of designers. You may view and compare the work record of designers in complete confidence and with no obligation. Or, if you prefer, or find it inconvenient to come to London, concise information on designers will be mailed to you by return post. You may specify the type of designer, the size of practice and geographic location.

The Register covers all areas of design expertise including: exhibition graphics, product and surface design.

Chartered Society of Designers, 29 Bedford Square, London WCIB 3EG (Tel: 01-631 1510)

SPECIMEN CONTRACT LETTER BETWEEN DESIGNER AND CLIENT

Designers who are members of the Chartered Society of Designers work to a code of professional conduct laid down by the Society and in their contract letter they will undertake to abide by this code.

Their letter will include the following points:

We undertake to carry out the design work involved in the .... exhibition for .... (client) at .... (venue) in accordance with the Code of Professional Conduct of the Chartered Society of Designers, a copy of which is enclosed.

Our fees will be in accordance with the scale of charges laid down for exhibition projects, payable as follows:

% on appointment
% on completion of work
% on final approval of all contractors'
accounts.

(Note: these percentages are subject to individual arrangements and agreements).

Contract letters can vary according to the project. Particular points will be raised within this letter.

A list of publications is available from Designer Publications Limited, the publishing company of the Chartered Society of Designers.

Source: Alan Taylor (Interpretation of SIAD Code)

COST ESTIMATING CHECKLIST

The Designers' Estimating Checklist will follow the earlier estimating checklist shown on pp. 134–5 but each section will be subdivided as necessary to highlight any special items.

Item	Estimated Cost
1. Direct Expenses	
Space costs	
Shell scheme – if applicable	
2. Exhibition Stand	
Construction	
Displays	
Photoprints	
Graphics	
Electrics	
Floor covering	
Furniture	
Floral	
Water and waste	
Compressed air/Hydraulics	
Telephone	
3. Design	
Model	
Visuals	
Working drawings	
Product display layouts	
Typographical layouts	
Visits to contractors	
Supervision on site	
Travelling expenses	
4. General	
Insurance	
Contingency	

Source: Collated by Alan Taylor

SPECIFICATION-WRITING CHECKLIST

The specification is intended to amplify the working drawings. In exhibition practice this follows the same general format – commencing at the floor and detailing all aspects to the roof of the stand, and then detailing specialist requirements.

1. NON-SHELL STAND

Floor treatment/platform
Check mark-out of stand and condition of floor. Lay carpet tiles to total area of stand.

or

Provide 100mm platform from standard floor panels, covered with carpet as sample provided, edged with 40mm aluminium trim.

Walls
Construct walls from standard 2.75m selected stock partitions to the heights and runs indicated on drawings. Finish all walls to the colours specified in emulsion paint.

Doors
Provide and fix all doors as indicated, complete with door furniture and locks with three sets of keys.

All doors to be finished gloss to the colours specified.

Fascia and Signs
Provide all fascia panels as indicated and signwrite lettering as detailed.

Roof
Provide and fix white muslin stretched taut to form roof.

Display areas/Panels
Provide all display treatment and panels as detailed on section drawing SD/1 and SD/2.

Receive all client's display exhibits and lay out as indicated.

On conclusion, repack all client's exhibits and re-crate and hand to client on stand for collection by client's transport.

Graphics

Prepare graphic panels as specified. Set all lettering to typographer's layouts and provide photoprints, mount and display as detailed.

Prepare matt photoprints of photographs from negatives provided, to the size shown. Wet-mount photoprints and wrap edges to 15mm ply panels and affix panels to display areas with split batten fixing. Cover all completed photoprints with polythene film for protection. Return panels to client upon completion.

Allow PC sum of £.... for all photographic work.

Floral

Provide, on hire, and fix floral boxes as shown and dress with floral decoration, not exceeding ....mm in height.

Decoration to be 50% seasonal flowers and 50% greenery.

Maintain daily throughout exhibition.

Furniture

Provide, on hire, furniture as listed on drawing WD3/1987.

Electrics

Provide all general and display lighting and power points as detailed on electrical drawing ED/1.

Water and Waste

Provide to office area, wash hand basin complete with water and waste connection.

Generally

All work to conform with the following working drawings:

WD1/1987

WD2/1987

WD3/1987

elevational drawings:

ELE/1

ELE/2

ELE/3

sectional drawings:

SD/1

SD/2

electrical details:

ED/1

Total drawings – 9

The requirements of the exhibition organisers' rules and regulations, and the statutory authorisation, must be observed in all work. The requirements of the Health and Safety Executive to be observed in all respects.

The work to be provided 'on hire' for the period of the exhibition, to be completed in all respects by noon the day preceding opening day, and all rubbish removed from site.

All work, plant and materials to be removed from site not later than 20.00hrs two days after the exhibition closing day, leaving the space in a clean and tidy condition.

Reference

Date

Tendering instructions are not normally included on the specification. These are on a separate document that is attached to the specification.

2. SHELL SCHEME

Shell stands provided by exhibition organisers normally contain all required basic items such as walls, floor coverings, fascia and nameboard. This is included in the prices quoted for such 'shell schemes'.

The additional items that the exhibitor needs to provide are:

Display panels or units
Alternative decorations or floor covering
Caption material
Floral displays
Electrical spotlights or other illuminations
Any other embellishment.

This is at the exhibitor's expense. Quite often an organiser will provide a range of additional items which are shown in his exhibitors' manual. These are normally competitively priced and well worth considering.

Alernatively, an exhibitor can have an 'interior display treatment' designed to be incorporated within the shell scheme.

Source: Alan Taylor

WORKING DRAWINGS FOR TENDERING

The exhibition stand building contractors rely on the specification and working drawings for preparing quotations. These are read together, one describing the work, the other illustrating it.

The working drawings need to show the following:

What the drawing shows	The drawing
1. The exhibition stand position in the hall	The site plan
2. The exhibition stand plan layout	Plan layout
3. One elevation should be provided for each exhibition frontage; two or three frontages would require two or three elevations	
4. Sectional drawings show sections through various parts of the stand where these are of a complex nature. Often several are needed.	Sections
5. Individual parts often need to be shown in detail. Sometimes but not always needed.	Details
6. Specialist plans show, for example: Electrical layouts Plumbing layout	Electrical layout Plumbing layout
7. Details of typography and photographs and caption matter are shown in layout form, usually half actual size, sometimes full size	Graphic layouts

Scales employed vary according to the size of the stand. Plan layouts are usually 1:200, a size most exhibition organisers prefer. The general rule is to use a convenient, legibly sized scale. The final result must show an accurate two-dimensional picture of the exhibition stand.

Construction of model

Models are often used. These are principally for the exhibitors' benefit since they allow planning of how best to utilise the stand, staff, and management training. They also show how colour can be used.

They have only limited value to the stand contractor since he requires finite details of constructional treatments which only working and section drawings can provide.

Source: Alan Taylor

EXHIBITION VENUE CONDITIONS

The owners of exhibition venues publish a list of conditions for the hire of their venues and exhibition organisers have to agree to observe these. They also have to undertake to ensure that their individual exhibitors conform with them.

These conditions are stated in the exhibition organisers' rules and regulations and also form part of the Application for Space which exhibitors complete.

The most notable mandatory items are:

- Care of the exhibition hall fabric and services
- Precaution against fire and flood
- Observance of statutory regulations and requirements
- Requirement to use the hall owners' electrical supply at certain stated rates, similarly his gas and water and waste services
- Requirements regarding Health and Safety Etc Act
- Requirements regarding the 'Exhibition Working Rule Agreement'
- Insurance requirements
- Fire and police requirements
- Any other local requirement or bye-law

These regulations are intended to protect the landlords' property, the general public, exhibitors and visitors.

These venue conditions run to many pages and requests can be made to any exhibition organiser for sight of them, if required.

SPECIMEN LETTERS BETWEEN DESIGNER AND CONTRACTOR(S)

1. Invitation to Contractor(s) to tender for work:

> Dear ....,
>
> Our client, the AB Company, is exhibiting at 'The Universal Trade Fair' to be held at the National Exhibition Centre, Birmingham, from 6 to 9 October 1987 in Halls 3 and 3a.
>
> We invite you to tender for the total stand-fitting work involved in accordance with the documents enclosed, namely:
>
> (a) Specification of works
> (b) Working drawings AB/1; AB/2; AB/3   (3)
> (c) Layouts LA/1; LA/2   (2)
> (d) Colour reference sheet
> (e) Exhibition rules and regulations
> (f) Furniture fabric and finishes – detail sheet
> (g) Envelope for return of your tender.
>
> All work is to conform with the rules and regulations of the exhibition, the requirements of the statutory authorities, and the requirement of the Health and Safety Executive.
>
> Your tender must be received not later than 21 days hence i.e. Monday 2 January, and must be sent in the envelope enclosed.
>
> All tenders will be opened at noon on that day, and our client's decision will be communicated to you within 14 days of that date.
>
> Our clients do not bind themselves to accept the lowest, or any tender.
>
> Yours sincerely,

2. Acceptance of Tender:

> Dear ....,
>
> Thank you for your quotation of (date) in respect of the AB Company Limited at the Universal Trade Fair to be held at the National Exhibition Centre, Birmingham.
>
> Our clients have instructed us to accept this tender and our official letter in respect of this work is enclosed.
>
> Our Mr Smith will be the designer responsible for this project and he will be sending you further copies of the drawings within the next few days. All contact should henceforth be through him.
>
> We look forward to working with your company to the successful completion of this contract.
>
> Yours sincerely,

3. Rejection of Tender:

> Dear ....,
>
> Thank you for submitting your quotation in respect of the AB Company Limited at the Universal Trade Fair to be held at the National Exhibition Centre, Birmingham.
>
> Our clients have accepted another quotation and we regret that we will not be asking you to carry out the work on this occasion, but we look forward to asking you to tender for future works.
>
> For your information, the tenders received for this work were as follows:
>
> £17,350
> £18,500
> £26,000
> £29,200
>
> The lowest tender has been accepted.
>
> Yours sincerely,

Source: Alan Taylor

EXHIBIT INFORMATION CHECKLIST SHEET

All products shown on the stand should be described in appropriate literature for visitors and intending buyers. Some products may be illustrated by photographs or models, which should also appear in appropriate literature.

A typical exhibit checklist:

Project:	Universal Trade Fair – National Exhibition Centre 18–27 October	
Date Required:	16 October 1989	
Department:	Publicity	
Exhibit/ Product	Type of Literature	Availability
1. Pumps (water) (All three sizes to be exhibited)	Brochure on three different pumps (number required – 4,000)	From stock – 10,000 available
2. Replacement parts	Manual of Parts (number required – 3,000)	From stock – 2,000 available. Place order for increased stock
3. New hoses	Leaflet (A4 single sheet) (number required – 6,000)	Prepare specially for exhibition
4. Manhole covers	Leaflet (2 fold A4) (number required – 8,000)	Prepare when final design is known (deadline 1 July 1989)
etc.	etc.	etc.

Deliver all literature to Mr Brown (Publicity Department) Exhibition Stand No. A123 on 16 October 1989 by own transport.

Source: Alan Taylor

GRAPHIC AND TOOL BAG CONTENTS FOR STAND MANAGER

Minor accidents often happen on an exhibition stand. Many of these can be quickly put right if the tools are available. A simple tool bag, carried by the stand manager, could comprise the following:

Joiner's hammer
Small display hammer
Wire-cutting pliers
Small hacksaw
Large screwdriver
Small electrical screwdriver
Ruler
1″ panel pins
$1\frac{1}{2}$″ panel pins
1″ oval nails
Selection of small screws, $\frac{3}{4}$″ to 2″
Evostick adhesive
Staple gun and staples
Assorted thin wire

For graphic requirements:

Set square
Pencils – 3H
Pentel pens
Masking tape
Velcro
Sticky pads
Scissors
Stanley knife and blades
Spray mount
Letraset sheets (assorted)
Tipp-Ex
Rubber
Sellotape
Double-sided Sellotape
Cow gum
A4 blank cards
Layout pads
Arrows (black, red and white)
Plenty of clean rags.

Sources:
Tool Bag – Alan Taylor
Graphic Bag – Brenda Lukey, Andry Montgomery Ltd

DESIGN INFORMATION: STANDARD EXHIBITION STRUCTURE STOCK SIZES

Exhibition stands are largely constructed from a collection of 'stock' items held by all stand contractors. These fall in two categories:

Traditional stock – normally to Imperial measurements

Modular stock – in Metric measurements

TRADITIONAL

Stock panels

These are either 9′ 0″ high (2.74m)
or 8′ 0″ high (2.5m)

Widths vary from 4′ 0″ down to 2′ 0″

'Make-up' panels are available at 12″ or 18″ widths. Any other size make-up panel has to be purpose made.

Stock panels are formed from a framework of 2″ × 1″ battens with two centre battens to provide a firm frame. Diagonal battens complete the stability. These 'frames' are faced either with hardboard or $\frac{3}{16}$″ ply panels, either on one side (single-sided panels) or both sides (double-sided panels).

Floor flats

Old stock consisted of 6′ 0″ × 2′ 0″ made up panels from 1″ timber planking laid on 3″ × 2″ joists which were laid on the exhibition hall floor. A small amount of this stock is still about.

New stock, which is widely used now, comprises sheets of $\frac{3}{4}$″ or 1″ chipboard which is either laid on 3″ × 2″ joists or, more commonly, cruciforms, which are small timber crosses laid under the chipboard sheets. This method is very fast and provides a very rigid floor.

The floor can either be 3″ or 4″ high depending on how the joists are laid.

The edge of the floor, or platform, is trimmed with either 3″ × 1″ or 4″ × 1″ boarding, which is painted to desired colour.

Fascias

Constructed as 2′ 0″, 1′ 6″ or 1′ 0″ deep. These are similar in construction to stock panels, but 2′ 0″ deep fascias, whilst fully faced on the outside face, are faced to only half the height on the inside to provide a recessed fixing for muslin ceilings.

Counters, Flower troughs, Doors

Most contractors carry stocks of these items but the standard sizes tend to vary.

Fascia supports

These are normally 2″ tubes with base plate and top fascia fixing. Some timber supports are still available.

MODULAR

A great many modular systems are now in general use and it is not possible to deal with every system. By and large they all work to a module of 1 metre width. The basic elements are:

Panels – normally 2.5 metres high by 1 metre width

Panel support tubes – normally 2.5 metres high by approximately 40mm thick.

Metal struts – to stabilise the stand – usually at roof level.

Fascias – normally about 300mm deep

Modular systems are rather like Meccano, and a great number of variations are possible from the available kit of parts.

Modular systems

An abridged list of some modular systems:
C.S.
Clip
Click
Consta
F. & T.
Gemini Staging
Marler Haley Exposystem
Meroform
Nimlock
Octanorm
Panelflex
Promedex
Rapid-ex
Syma
Zero

Sources: Alan Taylor, *Exhibition Bulletin* (List of Modular Systems)

READING DISTANCES

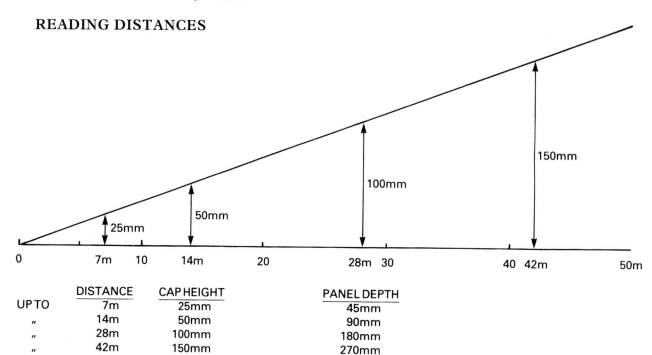

	DISTANCE	CAP HEIGHT	PANEL DEPTH
UP TO	7m	25mm	45mm
"	14m	50mm	90mm
"	28m	100mm	180mm
"	42m	150mm	270mm
"	84m	300mm	—
"	110m	400mm	—

Source: National Exhibition Centre signage manual

PROJECTION THROW

A great many factors influence this. Experts must be consulted if a perfect situation is to be achieved. Considerations include: room length, height, number of viewers, whether slides, film, back projection or video are to be shown.

The problems of low ceiling height are shown in Fig. A. Viewers should be limited in numbers.

Fig. B shows a ceiling height of 9′ 6″ (quite common). Head interference must be avoided by staggered seating. Rows should be no closer than 36″. Bottom edge of image should be 4′ 0″ above floor. Maximum screen size 5′ 0″ high × 7′ 5″ wide.

Fig. A

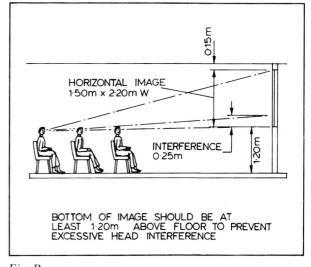

Fig. B

Source: A.V.E. Ltd

TYPICAL TWO-STOREY OR INTERMEDIATE HEIGHT STANDS

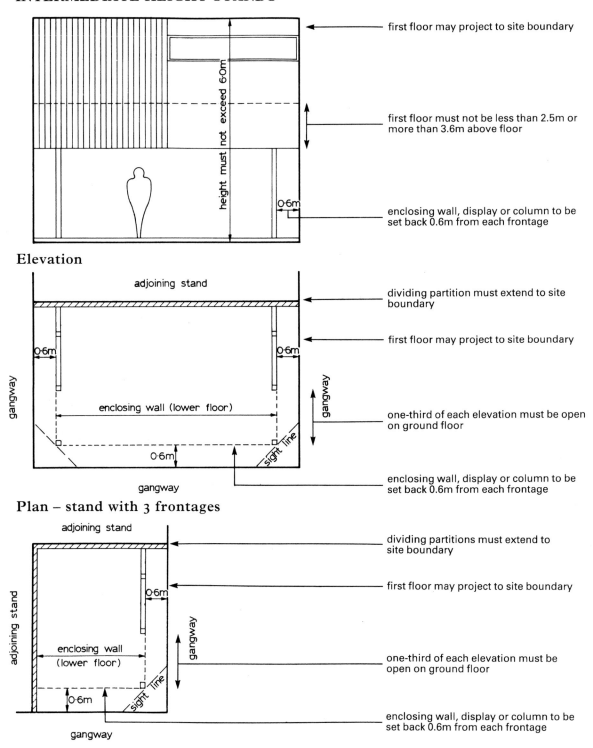

first floor may project to site boundary

first floor must not be less than 2.5m or more than 3.6m above floor

enclosing wall, display or column to be set back 0.6m from each frontage

Elevation

dividing partition must extend to site boundary

first floor may project to site boundary

one-third of each elevation must be open on ground floor

enclosing wall, display or column to be set back 0.6m from each frontage

Plan – stand with 3 frontages

dividing partitions must extend to site boundary

first floor may project to site boundary

one-third of each elevation must be open on ground floor

enclosing wall, display or column to be set back 0.6m from each frontage

Plan – stand with 2 frontages

Source: Interbuild Rules and Regulations

SIGN SIGHT LINES

As with all open choices the best solutions will be those which reduce the number of height lines to the minimum so that the eye can absorb and appreciate, even if unconsciously, the visual organization.

The fixing of signs can be broadly divided into side projecting, top hanging, flat mounted and free standing. The construction depends on the materials, but in form they might be flat panels, three-dimensional letters and internally illuminated boxes.

The merits of the various display methods is determined not only by their purpose and the environment in which they are to be displayed – that is to say ceiling heights, surface materials and so on – but also on sight lines, lighting incidence and traffic flow.

Lighting is an essential factor in the effective function of the sign and it may be necessary to increase this either with individual spot lights or by a generally higher level of illumination. Interior backlit signs have their own problems and will only be effective if they are made of the right materials, include the appropriate light fittings and enable easy replacement of lighting tubes.

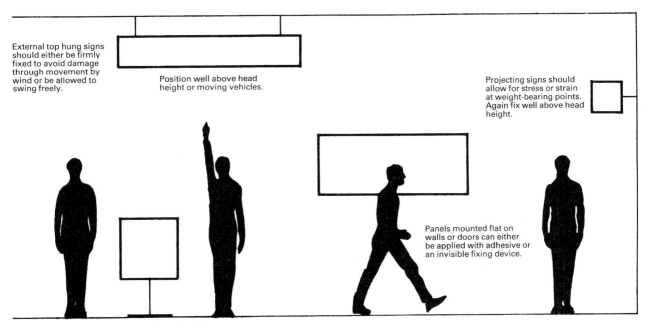

External top hung signs should either be firmly fixed to avoid damage through movement by wind or be allowed to swing freely.

Position well above head height or moving vehicles.

Projecting signs should allow for stress or strain at weight-bearing points. Again fix well above head height.

Panels mounted flat on walls or doors can either be applied with adhesive or an invisible fixing device.

Free-standing signs should be sufficiently light in weight to allow for manoeuvrability, but strong enough to prevent being knocked over.

PROOF CORRECTION MARKS

The following is a selection of marks recommended by the British Standards Institution. The full range can be obtained from BS 5261C:1976

Marginal mark	Meaning	Corresponding mark in text
♂ ⊢⊣	Delete (take out)	/ Cross through
⌐7 / ⊟	Delete and close-up	Above and below letters to be taken out
⊘	Leave as printed (when matter has been crossed out by mistake)	..... Under characters to remain
≡	Change to capital letters	≡ Under letters or words altered
=	Change to small capitals	= Under letters or words altered
≢	Change capitals to lower case	Encircle letters to be altered
≠	Change small capitals to lower case	Encircle letters to be altered
~	Change to bold type	~ Under letters or words altered
≈	Change to bold italic type	≈ Under letters or words altered
⊔⊔	Change to italics	___ Under letters or words altered
⊔⊔	Change to roman type	Encircle words to be altered
⊗	(Wrong fount.) Replace by letter of correct fount	Encircle letter to be altered
∩	Invert type	Encircle letter to be altered
×	Replace by similar but undamaged character or remove extraneous marks	Encircle letter to be altered
Ɣ	Insert (or substitute) superior figure or sign	/ or λ
∠	Insert (or substitute) inferior figure or sign	/ or λ
⊢⊣	Insert (or substitute) hyphen	/ or λ
⊢⊣	Insert (or substitute) rule	/ or λ (en or em etc.)
⊘	Insert (or substitute) solidus	/ or λ
...	Insert (or substitute) ellipsis	/ or λ
⊙	Insert (or substitute) leader dots	/ or λ
⊂	Close-up—delete space	⊂ Linking words or letters
Ɣ	Insert space		or Ɣ Between characters/words
Ⅰ	Make spacing equal		Between characters or words
⊤	Reduce space		or ⊤ Between characters/words
⊣c or ⊃⊢	Insert space between lines or paragraphs	
→ or ←	Reduce space between lines or paragraphs	

Marginal mark	Meaning	Corresponding mark in text
⊔⊓	Transpose	⊔⊓ Between letters or words, numbered when necessary
5	Transpose lines	5
[ ]	Place in centre of line	[ ] Around matter to be centred
(a)⊢⊏ ⊐ (b)⊏ ⊐⊣	Move to (a) the left, (b) the right	(a) ⊐ (b) ⊏
⌐	Begin a new paragraph	⌐ Before first word of new para.
⊇	No fresh paragraph here	⟶ Between paragraphs
⋋	(Caret mark.) Insert matter indicated in margin	⋋
⸌ ⸍ ⸜ ⸝	Insert single/double quotes	⋋ ⋋

FOREIGN LANGUAGE SPACE COMPARISONS IN PRINT

When converting captions and text to languages other than English, a greater amount of space should be allowed for. Generally, when the text is not technical, the following guide lines may be applied:

Language   *Additional space required*

Language	Additional space required
French	25% to 33%
German	33% to 50%
Italian	33%
Spanish	a generous 50%
Arabic	25%

NOTES:

Technical text is often shorter in German than in English.

Arabic typefaces can be similar in their space requirements to English typefaces and can require slightly less than 25% additional space. Advisable to consider type styles carefully.

Translations should always be made by a national of the country concerned.

Technical translations should always be made by a national versed in the technology concerned.

Source: Dick Negus, Negus Negus.

INTERNATIONAL PAPER SIZES

Exhibition printed matter should generally conform to the ISO paper size system. This is based on a constant ratio of $1:\sqrt{2}$ between width and depth.

The first diagram shows how posters, literature, letterpapers, forms, etc. fit into the ISO paper size system. The addition of one-third A4 and two-thirds A4 sizes for short letters, many forms, labels, pamphlets, etc. adds to the convenience and flexibility of the system.

It may be noted that the depth of each A size is identical with the width of the next larger size.

The second diagram shows how the three most common ISO envelope sizes relate to correspondence paper sizes.

Envelopes The DL (A4 folded twice) and C4 (A4 unfolded) are the most commonly used ISO envelope sizes. Remember that A4 paper already collated in a folder or manual may not fit in the standard A4 envelope but may need an oversize envelope.

Form sizes The trimmed sizes of forms should preferably conform to ISO paper sizes. Exceptions are items which need not be related to other than A4 filing requirements, and items which have limitations imposed by the dimensions of form-producing, form-feeding, or storing equipment.

Source: AML Design Manual

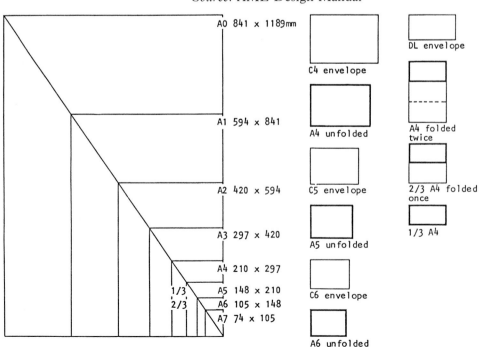

METRIC/IMPERIAL CONVERSION TABLES

The figures used in these conversions are to BS 350: Part 2: 1962

Some principal conversion factors are given below, and the tables opposite give detailed conversions for both imperial and metric measurements.

The bold figures in each table represent the unit to be converted. Its imperial equivalent is in the left-hand column, and the metric equivalent in the right – e.g. 1in = 25·400 mm, or 1mm = 0.03937in.

conversion factors

1in	=	25.4mm
1ft	=	30.48cm
1yd	=	0.9144m
1 mile	=	1.609 344km
1in²	=	6.451 6 cm²
1ft²	=	0.092 903 0 m²
	=	929.030 cm²
1yd²	=	0.836 127 m²
1in³	=	16.387 1 cm³
1ft³	=	0.028 316 8 m³
1yd³	=	0.764 555 m³
1 UK gal	=	4.545 96 litre
1lb	=	453.592 37 g
	=	0.453 59 kg
1 Btu/h	=	0.251 996 kcal/h
1mm	=	0.039 379 1 in
1cm	=	0.393 701 in
1m	=	39.370 1 in
1km	=	0.621 371 mile
1cm³	=	0.155 000 in²
	=	0.001 076 39 ft²
1m²	=	10.763 9 ft²
	=	1.195 99 yd²
1 cm³	=	0.061 023 7 in³
1m³	=	35.314 7 ft³
	=	1.307 95 yd³
1 litre	=	0.220 0 UK gal
1kg	=	2.204 62 lb
1 kcal/h	=	3.968 32 Btu/h

inches		millimetres
0.03937	1	25.400
0.07874	2	50.800
0.11811	3	76.200
0.15748	4	101.600
0.19685	5	127.000
0.23622	6	152.400
0.27559	7	177.800
0.31496	8	203.200
0.35433	9	228.600
0.39370	10	254.000
0.78740	20	
1.18110	30	
1.57480	40	
1.96850	50	
2.36220	60	
2.75591	70	
3.14961	80	
3.54331	90	
3.93701	100	
7.87402	200	
11.8110	300	
15.7480	400	
19.6850	500	
23.6220	600	
27.5591	700	
31.4961	800	
35.4331	900	
39.3701	1000	

feet		metres
3.2808	1	0.3048
6.5617	2	0.6096
9.8425	3	0.9144
13.1234	4	1.2192
16.4042	5	1.5240
19.6850	6	1.8288
22.9659	7	2.1336
26.2467	8	2.4384
29.5276	9	2.7432
32.8084	10	3.0480
65.6168	20	6.0960
98.4252	30	9.1440
131.234	40	12.1920
164.042	50	15.2400
196.850	60	18.2880
229.659	70	21.3360
262.467	80	24.3840
295.276	90	27.4320
328.084	100	30.4800

yards		metres
1.0936	1	0.9144
2.1872	2	1.8288
3.2808	3	2.7432
4.3745	4	3.6578
5.4681	5	4.5720
6.5617	6	5.4864
7.6553	7	6.4008
8.7489	8	7.3152
9.8425	9	8.2296
10.9361	10	9.1440
21.8723	20	18.2880
32.8084	30	27.4320
43.7445	40	36.5760
54.6807	50	45.7200
65.6168	60	54.8640
76.5529	70	64.0080
87.4891	80	73.1520
98.4252	90	82.2960
109.361	100	91.4400
546.807	500	457.200
1093.61	1000	914.400

square yards		square metres
1.1960	1	0.8361
2.3920	2	1.6723
3.5880	3	2.5083
4.7840	4	3.3445
5.9800	5	4.1806
7.1759	6	5.0168
8.3719	7	5.8529
9.5679	8	6.6890
10.7639	9	7.5251
11.9599	10	8.3613
23.9198	20	16.7225
35.8797	30	25.0838
47.8396	40	33.4451
59.7995	50	41.8064
119.599	100	83.6127

Fahrenheit		Celsius
32.0	0	−17.8
33.8	1	−17.2
35.6	2	−16.7
37.4	3	−16.1
39.2	4	−15.6
41.0	5	−15.0
42.8	6	−14.4
44.6	7	−13.9
46.4	8	−13.3
48.2	9	−12.8
50.0	10	−12.2
68.0	20	−6.7
86.0	30	−1.1
104.0	40	4.4
122.0	50	10.0
212.0	100	37.8

UK gallons		litres
0.2200	1	4.546
0.4400	2	9.092
0.6599	3	13.638
0.8799	4	18.184
1.0999	5	22.730
1.3199	6	27.276
1.5398	7	31.822
1.7598	8	36.368
1.9798	9	40.914
2.1998	10	45.460
4.3995	20	90.919
6.5993	30	136.379
8.7990	40	181.838
10.9988	50	227.298
13.1985	60	272.758
15.3983	70	318.217
17.5980	80	363.677
19.7979	90	409.136
21.9976	100	454.596

pounds		kilogrammes
2.2046	1	0.45359
4.4092	2	0.90718
6.6139	3	1.36078
8.8185	4	1.81437
11.0231	5	2.26796
13.2277	6	2.72155
15.4324	7	3.17515
17.6370	8	3.62874
19.8416	9	4.08233
22.0462	10	4.53592
44.0925	20	9.07185
66.1387	30	13.6078
88.1849	40	18.1437
110.231	50	22.6796
132.277	60	27.2155
154.324	70	31.7515
176.370	80	36.2874
198.416	90	40.8233
220.462	100	45.3592

Source: Building Trades Exhibition Limited, Interbuild Catalogue; and British Standards 350, Part 2, 1962

Source: Building Trades Exhibition Limited, Interbuild Catalogue; and British Standards 350, Part 2, 1962

ELECTRICAL SUPPLIES THROUGHOUT THE WORLD

Supplies vary in different countries and working exhibits will usually need transformers.

Commonly used voltages include:

200/100	400/230
220/127	415/240
240/120	440/250
380/220	600/347

If you do not know the voltage used in a particular country, check in a booklet published by the British Standards Institution, entitled *Survey of Supply Voltage Throughout the World*. The reference is TH20338 and it is available from the BSI at Milton Keynes.

NOTE: *Technical help to exporters (*THE*)*
For the past twenty years THE, a service of the British Standards Institution (BSI), has been investigating foreign markets and gathering information on technical legislation, practices and procedures, so as to make vital technical information directly available to exporters through a consultancy, information and publications service.

DISPLAY LAMP CATEGORIES

The lighting designer employs luminaries and lighting levels to highlight the display content of the stand, while at the same time ensuring that glare is avoided and that the environment is pleasant to be in without excessive heat.

A vast number of display lighting fitments is available. Certain manufacturers specialise and it is advisable to obtain their latest catalogues.

Generally, display lighting is categorised under the following headings:

Downlighter – recessed and surface mounted
High intensity discharge lamps
Gimbals – eyeball and lytecentre lamps
Halogen lights
Darklighters and multigroove – recessed and surface-mounted
Quadrilles – recessed, surface and wall-mounted
Spotlights and track lighting
Low voltage spotlights
Parabolic spotlights
Decorative fluorescent lighting

The Yellow Pages list names of lighting manufacturers, consultants and suppliers.

Three of the best known are:

Concord Lighting Limited
Concord House
241 City Road
London EC1V 1JD   Tel: 01-253 1200

Thorn EMI PLC
Thorn EMI House
Upper Street
St Martins Lane
London WC2   Tel: 01-836 2444

Philips
City House
420–430 London Road
Croydon
Surrey CR9 3QR   Tel: 01-689 2166

FLUORESCENT LAMP INFORMATION

Fluorescent lamps are available in a variety of sizes and lumen values.

Five of the main categories are shown below:

1. Fluorescent lamps 26mm (1in) diameter – energy saver switch start circuit operation.

    Sizes range from 600mm (2ft) length to 1500mm (5ft).

2. Fluorescent lamps 26mm (1in) diameter – switch start operation.

    Sizes range from 600mm (2ft) to 1500mm (5ft).

3. Fluorescent lamps 16mm ($\frac{5}{8}$in) diameter miniature – switch start operation.

    Sizes range from 150mm (6in) length to 525mm (21in).

4. Fluorescent lamps 38mm (1$\frac{1}{2}$in) diameter – standard.

    Sizes range from 600mm (2ft) length to 2400mm (8ft).

5. Circular fluorescent lamps. 300 and 400mm circumference.

Most fluorescent lamps are supplied in the following colours: white, cool white, warm white, daylight. Lumen values vary according to size.

Source: National Lighting Company Limited

COMMON DISPLAY PLANTS

A variety of decorative and foliage plants is generally available in most countries.

A recommended book on the subject is *Foliage House Plants*, published by Time Life International (Netherlands) BV, which illustrates the plants in colour.

The most common flowering plants are:

Chrysanthemum

Cyclamen

Poinsettia

Begonia

Pelargonium

Taller foliage plants available up to 6ft high (and taller in some cases) are:

Kentia Palm

Ficus Benjamina (weeping fig)

Hedera Canariensis (ivy)

Schefflera (umbrella plant)

Boston Fern

Monstera Deliciosa (cheese plant)

Rubber Plant

Yucca

Dracaena

Plants provided by floral contractors are 'on hire' for the period of the exhibition. Prices are determined either by the square metre for box arrangements, or by metre runs for troughs. Alternatively, a price is quoted for the total arrangement: this will be determined by density of flowers to greenery. A recommended split is 50/50, flowers to foliage. The plants are maintained daily by the contractor. Remember, the floral decorations are 'on hire' and exhibitors have no right to take them away at the conclusion of the exhibition without additional payment.

Source of plant information: International Exhibition Services Ltd.

SELECT BIBLIOGRAPHY

Books

Exhibitions – Universal Marketing Tools, Alfred Alles, Cassell

Going into Trade Fairs, International Trade Centre, UNCTAD/GATT

Trade Fairs and Exhibitions, Hugh A. Auger, Business Publications

Exhibitions International, Network

International Exhibition Handbook, National Trade Show Exhibition Association (USA)

Exhibition and Conference Year Book

Exhibition Trade Directory

The National Exhibition Centre, Edward D. Mills

The Architect as Stand Designer, David Dean, Scolar Press 1985

Exhibition and Display, Janice Gardner and Caroline Heller

Exhibition Design, Misha Black

Exhibition Design – Theory and Practice, Arnold Attenbury

The Protection of Industrial Designs, George Myrants

The Creative Handbook, The Creative Handbook Limited

The C.E.I. Services Directory, Conference and Exhibition Publications Limited

Booklets

Aggression in Recession, Association of Exhibition Organisers

Industry Profile, Association of Exhibition Organisers

BEPC Reviews:
Reaching the unknown prospect
The trade exhibition audience
The exhibitor and his approach to trade exhibitions
How trade exhibitions influence sales
Promoting trade exhibitions in the UK to Arab businessmen
Survey of trade fair/exhibition visitors to the UK during 1981
Exhibition bibliography

Guide for Exhibitors, Reg Best, Incorporated Society of British Advertisers

Exhibitions in Britain, Central Office of Information/British Overseas Trade Board

City of Birmingham Conference and Exhibition Handbook, City of Birmingham

Exhibition London, London Tourist Board

Exhibition Venue Specification, Association of Exhibition Organisers

BOTB's Service, British Overseas Trade Board

Trade Show Tips, H. B. G. Montgomery

Making Exhibitions Happen, Raymond F. Stock

Trade Exhibitions – How to Make the Most of your Investment

What Every Exhibitor Ought to Know, Interbuild Exhibitions/Video Arts

Investing in Success – How to Profit from Design Innovation, Christopher Lorenz

The BECA Exhibition Services Directory, British Exhibition Contractors Association

Society of Industrial Artists and Designers (now Chartered Society of Designers) publications:

Prospectus
Code of Professional Conduct
Working with your Designer
Interior Design – Conditions of Engagement

UK AND OVERSEAS EXHIBITION TRADE PRESS: CONTACTS AND ADDRESSES

UK

Alan Baker
The Editor
Conference Britain
Queensway House
2 Queensway
Redhill
Surrey RHI IOS

Peter Cox
The Editor
Conference World
Riverside House
High Street
Huntingdon
Cambridgeshire PE18 6SG

Robert Spalding
The Editor
Conference and Exhibitions International
Queensway House
2 Queensway
Redhill
Surrey RHI IQS

Ylva French
Destination London
World Trade House
145 High Street
Sevenoaks
Kent TN13 IXJ

J. S. Williams
The Editor
Exhibition Bulletin
266–272 Kirkdale
Sydenham
London SE26 4RZ

The Editor
Exhibition and Conference Factfinder
Pembroke House
Campsbourne Road
Hornsey
London N8 7PT

Owen Spence
The Editor
Exhibitions and Conferences
64 Brunswick Centre
Marchmont Street
London WCIN IAE

Austria

The Editor
Messemarkt Osterreich
Postfach 237
Jenullgasse 4
A 1141 Vienna

The Editor
Meeting Messe und Kongress Journal
Industriestrasse 2
A 2380 Perchtoldsdorf bei Wien

Belgium

The Editor
Europex
Foires et Expositions
Rue de La Longue Haie 52
B 1050 Brussels

Paul Aerts
The Editor
Foires et Expositions
Rue de Rochefort 106
B 5431 Wavreille

Canada

The Editor
Canadian Industry Shows and Exhibitions
481 University Avenue
Toronto M5W IA7
Ontario

France

The Editor
Expositions et manifestations
23 Rue de Courcelles
F 75362 Paris

M. Jean Dominique
Expo News Magazine
4 bis Rue Descombes
75017 Paris

Germany

Frau Stiege
The Editor
M + A Kalender
Postfach 101528
Grosse Eschenheimer Strasse 16
D 6000 Frankfurt/Main 1

The Editor
Messemagazin International
Achenbachstrasse 6
D 4000 Dusseldorf

The Editor
Messe und Kongress Vorschau
Postfach 1178
D 7750 Konstanz

Italy
The Editor
Fiere Nel Mondo
Centro Italiano Pubblicita
Via G Burzzesi 35
20146 Milan

Spain
The Editor
Ferias Y Congresos
Paris 149
Barcelona 9

Sweden
Marianne Frics
Masskalendern
Prastgaten 44B
S 111 29 Stockholm

Switzerland
The Editor
Schweizerische Messe-Revue
Villa Contessa
CH 6574 Vira Gamborogno

USA
Darlene Zonca
The Editor
Tradeshow Week
12233 West Olympic Blvd
Suite 236
Los Angeles CA 90064

The Editor
World's Fair
PO Box 339
Corte Madera
CA 94925

USEFUL ADDRESSES

General

AEO   Association of Exhibition Organisers
      207 Market Towers
      Nine Elms Lane
      London SW8 5NQ
      Tel: 01-627 3946

BECA British Exhibition Contractors' Association
      Kingsmere House
      Graham Road
      Wimbledon,
      London SW19 3SR
      Tel: 01-543 3888

CSD   Chartered Society of Designers
      29 Bedford Square
      London WC1 3EG
      Tel: 01-631 1510

      Exhibition Industry Federation
      207 Market Towers
      Nine Elms Lane
      London SW8 SNQ
      Tel: 01-627 5722

UFI   Union des Foires Internationales
      35 bis Rue Jouffroy,
      Paris 75017
      Tel: (1) 4267 9912

LEVA London Exhibition Venues Association
      c/o Denise McKenzie
      Press Office
      Earls Court Exhibition Centre
      Warwick Road
      London SW5 9TA
      Tel: 01-385 1200

ISBA Incorporated Society of British Advertisers
      44 Hertford Street
      London W1Y 8AE
      Tel: 01-499 7502

      The Association of British Chambers of Commerce
      Sovereign House
      212a Shaftesbury Avenue
      London WC2H 8EW
      Tel: 01-240 5831

      The Design Council
      28 Haymarket
      London SW1
      Tel: 01-839 8000

RIBA   Royal Institute of British Architects
66 Portland Place
London W1
Tel: 01-580 5533

BTA   British Tourist Authority
64 St James's Street
London SW1
Tel: 01-499 9325

DTI   Department of Trade & Industry
1–19 Victoria Street
London SW1H OET
Tel: 01-215 7877

The British Council
10 Spring Gardens
London SW1A 2BN
Tel: 01-930 8466

BSI   British Standards Institution
2 Park Street
London W1A 2BS
Tel: 01-629 9000

BT   British Telecom
2–12 Gresham Street
London EC2V 7AG
Tel: 01-357 3000

COI   Central Office of Information
Hercules Road
London SE1 7DU
Tel: 01-928 2345

Video Arts Ltd
Film Production
68 Oxford Street
London W1
Tel: 01-637 7288

Exhibition halls

Earls Court and Olympia Limited
Warwick Road
London SW5 9TA
Tel: 01-385 1200

Barbican Centre
Barbican
London EC2Y 8DS
Tel: 01-588 8211

Alexandra Palace & Park
Wood Green
London N22 4AY
Tel: 01-883 6477

Wembley Conference and Exhibition Centre
Wembley
Middlesex HA9 ODW
Tel: 01-902 8833

Kensington Exhibition Centre
99 Kensington High Street
London W8 5TD
Tel: 01-937 9898

National Exhibition Centre
Birmingham B40 1NT
Tel: 021-780 4171

Scottish Exhibition and Conference Centre
Glasgow G3 8YW
Tel: 041-221 1769

The Greater Manchester Exhibition and Events
Centre
Manchester M1 6FQ
Tel: 061-834 2700

The Brighton Metropole
The Brighton Metropole Hotel
Kings Road
Brighton BN1 2FU
Tel: 0273-775432

Harrogate International Centre
North Yorkshire HG1 5LA
Tel: 0423-68051

Glossary

Like most industries, the exhibition industry has its own vocabulary. The following is a selection of the most commonly used words and phrases. Particular country of usage is indicated in each case by (UK) or (USA). If there is no such indication the word is in common usage in both the UK and the USA.

A sizes Also known as DIN sizes. A series of standard paper sizes which normally range from Ao (841 × 1189mm) to A7. The ratio between the long and the short sides is the same throughout the range and any A sheet folded in half across its long dimension and cut along that fold produces two sheets of the next smaller size in the range. This range of paper sizes is used throughout the world with the exception of the USA, where the imperial sizes are still used.

Acetate Film positive or negative from which silkscreens are produced. Also a family of plastics for light transmission and surface protection.

Acrylic The family of clear, colour and translucent thermo-plastic resins such as Plexiglas or Lucite (USA), Perspec (UK).

Acrylic emulsion A water-based latex paint made of acrylicpolymer.

Adjustable standard Vertical support which allows shelf bracket to be affixed at any point in its length (USA).

Adlux A black and white photo transparency (USA).

Affixed merchandise Client's products fixed to display (USA).

Aisle Area for audience traffic movement. Also 'Gangway'.

Ambient light Existing uncontrolled illumination, normally applied to daylight.

Animation Movement of light or mechanical action (models, diagrams, etc); or cartoon film technique.

Anti-stat wax/cream Solution applied to plastics, particularly acrylics, to minimise dust accumulation.

Arch A display ceiling which spans two points (USA).

Artwork A mounted assembly of graphics prior to reproduction, usually on heavy-duty card.

Audience Term usually applied to the visitors to a particular exhibition, or the people your exhibit is aimed at.

Audio General term applied to anything to do with sound.

Audiovisual (AV) A technique using sound and light to convey a message. Also the equipment used for this purpose.

Axonometric A perspective-like drawing except that all lengths are to scale, drawn on two axes at 45 degrees to the vertical. (*See also* Isometric.)

Backlining (UK). *See* Countermount.

Back-to-back Stands sharing a common back wall (UK).

Backwall Panel arrangement at rear of exhibit area (USA).

Balancer *See* Backlining.

Banner A suspended decorative or communicative panel (USA). A graphic sign made of fabric (UK).

Batten A piece of square-sawn softwood timber (UK).

Bed hook Metal hardware in pairs (female and male) used for inserting into panel edge to permit easy coupling of panels (USA).

Black-light Ultra-violet lighting that causes phosphorescent paint to glow.

Bleed Area beyond usable section of graphics which allows for trimming or wrapping of finished print.

Blockboard A core of edge-glued timber with a thin lamination of face veneer on either side (UK). Resin impregnated solid, no warp knots etc.

Blow-up The enlargement of a two-dimensional item by photography.

Blue print (USA). *See* Dyeline.

Blue sky Term for extreme design or thinking (USA).

Body copy/text A block of works as opposed to a heading or other single line or words. Usually applied to display text.

Booth The American word for exhibit stand (USA).

Break down 1. Term used to describe dismantling period of an exhibition.
2. An itemised estimate or quotation of costs for producing an exhibit.

Brief Detailed instructions or outline information provided to the designer by his client.

British Standard Colours Standard paint colours made by all major manufacturers to British Standard 4800: 1972 (UK).

Bromide A black and white photograph (UK).

'Brush hand' Slang term for painter (UK).

Build up 1. The erection period and setting up time required to produce a finished exhibit (UK).
2. A system of programming flasher to light lamps in cumulative sequence with time intervals between (USA).

Butt To join or align edge to edge.

Buyer's Guide *See* Catalogue.

B X Cable Flexible armoured electrical cable accepted as insulated by most codes; two, three or more wires (USA).

Call-out Notation on drawings or exhibits of special significance, i.e. finish, edge, colour detail or features (USA).

Cap-height The height of a capital letter (mm in UK, ins in USA). Used in specifying the height of letterform to be used.

'Caps' A contraction of 'capital letters'.

Carcase The load bearing part of a structure, in exhibition work usually a box-like timber frame.

Casement Fabric used for ceilings and display draping, a better quality muslin (UK).

Catalogue Detailed listing of all exhibitors with addresses, telephone numbers, telex etc. who are exhibiting in a particular exhibition. Of particular use to exhibition visitors as a reference source after the exhibition has finished.

'Chippie' Slang term for carpenter or joiner (UK).

Circuit 1. A complete pattern or group of exhibitions on related subjects.
2. Electrical.

Circulation The flow of people around an exhibition.

Circus 1. An exhibition full of clowns.
2. *See* Circuit.

Cladding Surface panels applied to carcase or other structural frame.

Client The person commissioning designers and contractors, etc.

Closer Panel to fill in gap between two stands, or disguise blank spaces.

Comp Comprehensive layout or design (USA).

Conduit Metal, plastic or fibre tube fitted to wall, ceiling or under platform of exhibit used as an encasement for electrical leads.

Conservation (conservator) Repair and preservation of objects. The person who carries out conservation is known as a conservator. Particularly applies to museums and archive material.

Consolidate The process of gathering together exhibition stands within the exhibition hall to eliminate unsold spaces. Normally carried out by the exhibition organiser at a very late stage in planning.

Contingency Sum of money allowed in estimate or as a p.c. item, to cover any unforeseen expenses. Often this is listed as a percentage (usually 10–15%) of the total cost of the project as estimated.

Contractor Company contracted to build an exhibition stand.

Copy The words that are to appear in any graphics on the exhibit.

Copy negative Film negative made from glossy print or other artwork for production of additional prints.

Corporate identity The visual expression of a company, encompassing its vehicle livery, uniforms, and factory/office environment as well as its graphics.

Countermount Technique for mounting material to rear of panel to prevent the face-mounted material on the same panel causing warping (USA). Called 'Backlining' in UK.

Craneage Lifting, normally using a crane or other special equipment (UK).

Cubic content The use of exhibit properties in the air space over the booth area to a height of eight feet or more (USA).

Custom exhibit An exhibit which is a unique solution to the specific requirements of the user, i.e. not a shell scheme (USA).

Cutting sheet Sheet of full-size drawings made by contractor, detailing size and shape of raw material to be cut (USA).

'Daily News' or 'Bulletin' News sheet issued by exhibition organisers to exhibitors at an exhibition.

Datum points Permanent points marked on the floor of the exhibition hall which are used by the exhibition organisers in laying out exhibitions.

Decks Term applied to floors of exhibit, normally those above ground level.

Decor The interior decoration of a stand (USA).

Demonstrator Person on exhibition stand who presents merchandise or exhibit to visitors.

Designer Person employed by exhibitor to design (and occasionally to supervise) his stand.

Detail Construction drawing which shows exact method of construction or specific construction features.

Didactic Educational theory. Also called 'Thematic'.

Dilapidations The making good of any damage to the exhibition hall floor or wall caused by contractors or others (UK).

Diorama A dimensional representation in forced perspective normally viewed through a small rectilinear opening which controls the viewing angles.

Display The exhibiting of objects, also applies to the way in which the actual exhibits are presented.

District surveyor Surveyor employed by local authority from whom it is necessary to get approval of all substantial structures used in exhibition halls (UK).

Dolly Any of several kinds of low, flat, wheeled frames for transporting heavy exhibits (USA).

Double-decker An exhibition stand which has ground floor and first floor levels.

Double-sided tape Adhesive tape with adhesive on both front and rear faces used for mounting graphics, light-weight exhibits etc.

Drapes Curtains or other fabric hangings (USA).

Drayage Handling of exhibit properties between exhibition hall loading dock and exhibit area (USA).

Drayman Official show handler designated to move exhibits from loading dock to exhibit area (USA).

Dressed lumber Timber which has been sanded or smoothed down to less than its rough dimensions (USA).

Dresser *See* Window dresser.

Drop slot Opening in counter top to receive cards (USA).

Drop wire Method of supporting exhibit or lights from above, normally a wire dropped from the roof structure of the exhibition hall.

Dyeline Copy of working drawing produced from translucent original (UK).

'E & D' Erection and dismantling (USA).

Easel A stand or frame for displaying objects, or a blackboard.

Elevations Front and side views of exhibit, normally on scaled drawing.

Enclosure Area within the exhibit that is shut off from it and normally consists of such areas as office, store cupboard etc.

Erection Assembling of exhibit on site.

Estimate Approximate calculation of exhibit costs, normally prior to commitment.

Exhibit 1. A term meaning exhibition or a series of displays (USA).
2. A single unit within an exhibition, e.g. a display case, a product, etc. (UK).

Exhibition A series of displays (or, in UK, exhibits) dealing with a particular theme. In USA this term has the same meaning as 'exhibit' although often it is used to cover a much larger event.

Exhibition Manager *See* Show Director.

Exhibitor The company which exhibits.

Exhibitor Stand Manager Person with overall responsibility for the running of a particular exhibit. Normally employed by the Exhibitor. Also Exhibit Manager (USA).

Exhibitor's manual Compendium containing rules and regulations, deadlines and other vital information issued by the exhibition organiser to each individual exhibitor.

Extras Additional items provided by the contractor or others outside the scope of the original contract.

F.S. An abbreviation of the term 'full-size', which indicates on a drawing that the item shown has been drawn at exactly the same size as the actual drawing.

Fabrication The building or construction of an exhibit or display (USA).

Fascia A wide board over the front face of an exhibit site normally carrying the name of the exhibitor and the stand number. Called 'header' in USA.

Feature A prominent or eye-catching display.

Field services Handling installation and dismantling including freight, drayage, carpentry, electrical, plumbing, ironworkers, riggers and maintenance (USA).

Finishes Materials such as felt, paint, plastic laminate, etc. applied to cladding to complete the basic structure of an exhibit.

Fire Officer Local official responsible for ensuring that all the necessary fire regulations are met.

Fire proofing/retardant Term used to describe a finish, usually liquid, which coats materials with a fire resistant cover. This does not render the material fireproof, merely inhibits the spread of flame if there is a fire.

Flame-proofed Term used to describe material which is, or has been treated to be, fire-retardant.

Flat A panel made from sheet material (such as plywood) framed with timber on the rear face, double-sided.

'Flier' Slang for getting a quick start on the building of an exhibit (UK).

Flier Piece of print to announce news, such as participants in an exhibition.

Flood/Floodlight A tungsten lamp with a built-in reflector which gives a broad, soft-edged beam of light.

Floor flaps *See* Platforms.

Floor Manager The exhibition manager, the organiser's representative actually in the exhibition hall dealing with on-site problems.

Fluorescent Light provided from a gas-filled tube. (Slang name – 'fluories' (UK)).

Flush mount Mounting one material to another with no space between.

Free-standing Self-supporting or independent exhibit material.

Frontage The side of the exhibit facing the gangway.

GRP Glass-reinforced polyester. Also known under the trade name of 'Fibreglass'.

Galley proof Body text set in one long run to measure specified, and supplied by typesetters for checking before being cut up to produce artwork or correct layout. The first stage as received from the typesetter and the prime time to check for mistakes.

Gangway *See* Aisles.

'Ghoster' Slang term applied to nightworking.

Glass, non-reflective Glass treated to give matt surface to minimise reflected light.

Glass painting Illustration painted on several parallel sheets of clear glass to give three-dimensional effect.

Glossy Common term for black and white photograph reproduced on glossy paper.

Grain of wheat General term for miniature lamps, usually 4 volt or under (USA).

Graphics Two-dimensional material made up of illustrations and text etc.

Greenfield (USA). *See* Conduit.

Groundwork The three-dimensional modelled surface at the front of a diorama (UK).

Groupage Collecting individual freight items and shipping collectively.

Guestimate Estimate not based on factual calculation.

Gutter Space between facing pages allowing for stitching fold etc.

Half-tone Term used to describe reproduction technique of photographing full tone artwork through a dot screen so that all blacks and greys acquire values as a result of dot density. Used as a means of reproducing full-tone art-work for printing.

Hall dressing Presentation of overall look of exhibition to bring cohesion to the exhibition.

Hall Manager The exhibition hall owner's representative on site.

Header (USA). *See* Fascia.

Heat sealing The application of a very thin sheet of either glossy or matt plastic over graphic panels to protect them from dirt, finger prints etc.

'Heavy gang' Slang term for the people who move exhibits.

Horizontal show An exhibition with no restriction on the nature of goods displayed.

Hot spots Condition caused by proximity of light source to transparency diffuser etc. when a halo of bright light is produced instead of even illumination.

Inserts 1. Loose-leaf print in catalogue etc. 2. Interchangeable copy on graphic panels.

Installation The final setting-up of exhibits within the stand.

Instructions Directions issued by designer to contractor, usually after the contract has been placed, covering additional or altered work. It is usually necessary for the contractor to receive a written instruction from the designer to validate any extra charges that he may want to include in his final invoices to the client.

Internegative A film negative made from transparency or other positive original to use in making additional positive copies.

'Iron fighters' Slang for metal workers (UK).

Island site A display that may be viewed from gangways on all sides. A stand open on all four sides.

Isometric A perspective-like drawing except that all lengths are to scale drawn on two axes at 60 degrees to the vertical.

Itinerant A re-usable exhibit or display with scheduled shipping from place to place (USA).

Jig Shop or bench set-up making repetitive assemblies.

'Juice' Slang term for electricity.

Justification The arrangement of type with letter spacers to give lines of equal length. (*See also* Range left/right.)

KD **(knockdown)** Exhibit or display components requiring assembly on site.

Labourer (UK)/**Laborer** (USA) Unskilled helper.

Landscape Photograph, panel or exhibit having the longer dimension in the horizontal plane.

Layout (Exhibition) Floor plan of exhibition.

Layout (Graphic) Full size sketch layout of finished graphics prior to typesetting and client approval.

Leading The spaces between the lines of type-setting. The width of this space is a major factor in the readability of long sequences of text.

Light box Enclosure with lighting and translucent face of plastic or glass, usually with graphics applied to surface or film transparency sandwiched between translucent and clear (face) sheets.

Line negative A special photographic negative that will only accept black or white and not tones. Especially useful in the reproduction of text, wood engravings, etc.

Linework A graphic in black and white without any intermediate grey tones, it can be reproduced in any one colour without the use of a half-tone screen and because of this it is much cheaper to reproduce than a graphic with a complete range of tones.

'Logo' **(Logotype)** A trademark or symbol usually unique to an exhibitor's company.

Loop projector Film projector modified to run film which has been spliced into a continuous loop.

Mark-up 1. The layout, normally using chalked strings, of the exhibition hall floor to indicate individual exhibitors' sites.
2. Instructions for typesetters on particular setting required for copy.
3. Extra charge on bought-in goods.

Master The artwork or original from which copies are made.

Measure The maximum width of a text area or a single line of text.

Message repeater Device with recorded tape in cartridge form, used to repeat recording continuously or on call.

Mobile An art form suspended or balanced with freedom of movement.

Mobile exhibit A free-moving exhibit that may need restraining for safety purposes.

Mock-up A scale model of an exterior showing colours, area etc.

Model 1. A full-scale model of proposed structure.
2. A live person displaying clothing.

Modular display systems Off-the-shelf exhibit systems using a number of repeating elements.

Monochrome A graphic image of only one colour.

Montage A display using an artistic arrangement of many individual parts superimposed on each other.

Mounting (Dry/Wet) The mounting of flat material onto support panels, walls, etc. either using heat-activated adhesive (dry mounting) or liquid paste (wet mounting).

Muslin A wide-loomed fabric used for ceilings and other display work. *See also* Casement.

Nameboard *See* Fascia.

Negative A reverse print or photographic original.

Negotiated contract A contract and price agreed with one nominated contractor without tendering.

Night sheets Protective sheeting placed around frontage of exhibit during exhibition hall closed hours to guard against theft, dust or competitors.

Nominal sizes (UK). *See* Dressed lumber.

Nominated contractor Contractor chosen without going out to general tender. Usually on a regular basis.

Official contractors Service organisations appointed by show organisers.

One ten/sixty Common term describing normally available current in North American continent: 110v, 60 cycles (USA).

Organiser Person or group instigating and supervising exhibition.

Overlay A flap, usually of transparent or translucent material, over an original graphic giving special instructions to the printer or other graphic producer (UK). Also:

Overlay (USA)/**Overmount** (UK) A panel mounted on top of another surface.

PAR Or 'parabolic'. Common term for sealed beam spot or floor lamp with self-contained lens surface glass, which provides a precisely controlled high-intensity beam of light. Also a low voltage spot.

p.c. sum Prime cost sum. An actual amount of money specified in the tender documents by the designer, which the contractor adds to his quotation. Often used to cover items of which insufficient details are known at tender stage. In the final invoice the contractor would charge the actual cost of any p.c. sums.

PMT 'Photo mechanical transfer' – a means of producing a print direct from a piece of artwork or another print without going via a negative. The process is particularly useful in that any scale changes can be easily made between the original and the resulting PMT print.

Paste-up *See* Artwork.

Pea lamps (UK). *See* Grain of wheat.

Performance cone The area of effective light obtained from a light fitting.

Photo blow-up Photographic reproduction in larger size than original.

Photostat A reproduction process employing paper negatives.

Pin-up Light fixture with surface mounting plate or with clamp base (USA).

Pipe Scaffold-like structure used to support curtains dividing individual exhibit areas (USA).

Plan A top view scale drawing.

Planting The provision of flowers and foliage on the exhibit.

Plates Metal sheets to spread heavy loads.

Platform A modular system of timber platforms, usually four inches in height, used to create the raised floor of an exhibit (UK).

Plywood, lumber core *See* Blockboard (USA).

Podium A stand-up demonstration area.

Portable display An itinerant exhibit capable of being carried by one man (USA).

Portrait A photograph, image or graphic panel having the longer dimensions in the vertical plane.

Preliminary sketches Idea sketches preceding proposals by the designer.

Press kit Compendium of information on your company and exhibit prepared for giving out to the press.

Press preview Opening of the exhibition, usually one or two days before the official opening to the public or trade, to allow press access.

Preview Article, sometimes a complete supplement, in trade press or other publications, issued prior to the opening of the exhibition.

Proof Any preliminary reproduction by photography or typesetting etc. provided for approval prior to finished product.

Prop Any display item used to enhance the exhibit other than the exhibitor's products.

Public show An exhibition that is open to the general public.

'Punters' Slang name applied to exhibition workmen (UK).

Pylon A tall exhibit structure normally used for identification.

Quotation A definite price provided by a contractor for carrying out a specified project.

Rail A low divider between exhibits (USA).

Range left/right Type that is aligned to the left or right. *See also* Justification.

Rear projection Film, slide or filmstrip presentation where the screen is between the viewer and the projector.

Refurbish To brighten, freshen, renovate. Usually during the run of a show.

Register The exact alignment of two or more printed images usually achieved by the producer lining up specially provided register marks on each of the original images.

Regulations The official conditions applied to an exhibitor by the organiser and hall owner.

Return Common term for a panel joined to another at a 90 degree angle.

Reveal Common term for side portion of panel or structure visible to audience.

Reverse left to right To make a photographic image face in the opposite direction by turning the negative over in the enlarger when printing.

Reverse-out To produce white text against a dark background photographically by placing a positive image in the enlarger with the negative image of the background photograph.

Review Press report on exhibition after the event.

Rigger 1. General construction worker on exhibition site (USA).
2. Specialist who fixes drop wires and other construction at extreme heights, e.g. from the roof of the exhibition hall (UK).

Riser (USA). *See* Platform.

Rollers Method of moving heavy loads, using tubular rollers.

Roller coat Technique for applying paint with rollers, rather than brushes, usually used with latex or vinyl based paints (USA).

Rough sketch Quick drawing giving indication of proposed exhibit. *See also* Layout.

Rubber back Type of carpet with built-in underlay.

S/S 1. In exhibition work an abbreviation that means site size and refers to the complete visible area of an image or exhibit (e.g. with a framed picture, the area of that picture including the frame).
2. In graphic work an abbreviation generally accepted as meaning same size (i.e. artwork that is to be reproduced the same size as the original artwork presented to the contractor).

Sandwich A sheet of clear glass or acrylic with a second sheet of opaque glass or acrylic beneath it, between which is sandwiched a film or paper graphic. Used to produce the top sheet of a light-box.

Satin finish Smooth semi-gloss finish usually on a metal or lacquered surface.

Scene in action Term for mechanical animation technique which achieves simulated flow motion by rotating striped cylindrical acetate drum between light source and face artwork (USA).

Scribe Technique of fitting pre-fabricated unit into existing site condition by cutting pre-fabricated unit slightly to allow perfect fit.

Secret fixing Method of applying object to background with no visible means of support. *See also* Split batten.

Section Working drawing representing the elevation of an imaginary plane cutting through the exhibit or other object, usually in a vertical plane.

Self-contained exhibit A display which is an integral part of its own shipping case (USA).

Sepia Brown-tinted photographic reproduction from black and white negative. Normally costs approximately twice as much as straight black and white print.

Services General term applied to electric, gas, compressed air, water, waste and other such services provided in exhibition hall (UK). *See also* Utilities.

Setter-out The contractor's draftsman who produces rods (UK) or otherwise sets out the full-scale drawings for the carpentry shop.

Set-up Assembly of exhibits for review or use (USA).

Set-up drawing The plans from which the exhibit components are assembled.

Sheets *See* Night sheets.

Shell scheme Modular system of exhibit booths provided by the organiser for the exhibitor. Usually consists of floor covering, back and side walls, ceiling, fascia panel and other basic structure and services.

Shell stand Term used to describe stand within overall exhibit shell scheme.

Shop drawings *See* Cutting Sheet.

Showcase General term for glazed or framed enclosure for displaying exhibits or objects.

Show Director Person within exhibition organiser's office in ultimate control of exhibition (USA).

Sight lines The views of an exhibit or exhibition as seen by the visitor.

Silk screen Method of applying graphics by printing through a fine stencil supported on silk stretched within a frame; printing ink is pushed through the stencil using a squeegee. The process requires a positive film to produce the necessary graphics for printing. Particularly useful as printing can be carried out on almost any material.

Site General term applied to location of exhibition.

Site plan *See* Layout (Exhibition).

s.j. cord Rubberised electric cable commonly used as a flexible lead or when conduit or greenfield are not practical (USA).

Sketch model A three-dimensional, simple block model usually made by the designer to indicate general layout of proposed exhibit. Often used instead of or with a visual.

'Sky-hooks' Slang term used by construction workers and contractors to indicate a structure proposed by the designer or his client which has no practical means of support.

Soffit A lowered portion of a ceiling.

Space Term applied to site area of exhibit.

'Sparks' Slang term for electricians (UK).

Specialist Term used to describe supplier or manufacturer who is an expert in a particular field, outside the normal run of services provided by contractors.

Specification Document produced by designer as part of tender documentation to outline details of working, quality control, insurances, responsibilities and all other matters concerning the proposed contract which are not adequately covered by the information on the working drawings.

'Spikes' Slang term for large nails (UK).

Split batten A horizontal piece of timber cut in two at 45 degrees; one half is fixed to the back of a panel or exhibit, the other to a wall. The panel is then hung on the wall so that one half of the timber fits over the other.

Spot (light) Lamp providing controlled circle of light from tungsten source, with built-in reflector. *See also* Flood.

Stand Term applied to individual exhibit booth (UK).

Stand fitter *See* Contractor.

Stand Manager *See* Exhibition Stand Manager. Exhibit Manager (USA).

Standing orders Officially approved list of requirements for exhibit workers, covering the methods of working and requirements on site.

Staples Term applied to special clips used by electricians to hold electrical cables in correct position (UK).

Stat *See* Photostat.

Steward Workers' trade union representative on site, also known as shop steward (UK).

Stock panels Standard framed panels available from contractor's stock on hire for construction of exhibit walls, etc. (UK).

Storyboard Complete written outline of proposed exhibit including final text and word descriptions of all graphics and exhibits to be used. Normally produced by the designer for the client.

Stretcher Tool used in carpet laying.

Stud Vertical structural wall support of wood or metal.

Studio Artist's and signwriter's workplace.

Studio hands The people who work in a studio (applicable to artists and signwriters only) (UK).

Sub-contractor Specialist contractor who is contracted to do specific parts of the work by the main contractor, who is normally responsible for the sub-contractor's work within his own contract.

'Sweepers' Slang term for exhibition cleaners (UK).

Switchgear General term applied to main electrical switches and fuse box, etc.

Symbol A distinctive design by which an organisation is identified.

System build An exhibition built with a proprietary display system.

'T & M' An abbreviation of a form of billing through labour costs ('time and materials') (USA).

'Tacker' Slang name for carpet layer (UK).

Tacks Name given to small nails (UK).

Talking head A mannequin onto which a film of facial features is projected to give the impression, with a sound track, that the mannequin is talking.

Target audience/population The group for which an exhibit or other medium is eventually intended.

Template Pattern or guide used to produce various repetitive items. Also often used to ensure a particular exhibit will actually fit into or onto the plinth, etc., being made for it.

Tender Written quotation supplied by contractor, based on information contained within tender documents.

Tender documents Usually, complete set of working drawings and specification outlining the work required by the designer from the contractor for the production of a particular exhibit. These documents are normally used as the basis for competitive tenders between various contractors so that the client can decide which contractor is best, on the basis of identical information provided to each contractor.

Text The actual words that are to appear on the graphics in the exhibit.

Thematic *See* Didactic.

Touch-up The final cleaning and re-touching of painted surfaces to ensure an absolutely perfect finish for the opening and during the exhibition. Also applies to small amounts of the paints used to paint a particular exhibition stand, which are kept with the exhibit for the purpose of touching up any nicks or scratches during the run of the exhibition.

Trade show An exhibition which is only open to people involved in a particular trade or industry, not to the general public.

Traffic flow A supposed or directed path the visitors will take through an exhibit.

Transparency A black and white or coloured transparent or translucent photograph.

Traveller A heavy-duty traverse rod to support drapes (USA).

Treble decker An exhibition stand on three levels.

Turntable Electrically or manually rotated platform.

'Two by one' Slang term applied to two inch by one inch (25mm × 50mm) timber (UK).

'Two forty volts' Common terms describing normally available current in UK. 240 volt 50 hertz (cycles) (UK).

Typesetting The operation of transforming words into printed letter form using either hot metal, photographic or typewritten processes.

Un-justified An arrangement of type or lettering where spaces between letters are constant and as a result all lines are of a different length. *See also* Justified.

Utilities (USA). *See* Services.

Variations Term applied to any changes to original instructions to contractor. *See* Instructions.

Velarium An awning or shelter over the top of an exhibit, usually applied to fabric ceilings.

Venue The site location of an exhibition.

Vertical show An exhibition confined to goods in a particular industry or to allied goods.

Video General term applied to television programmes, or graphics displayed on a television receiver. (The receiver is often known as a VDU – 'visual display unit').

Visitor Person visiting the exhibition.

Visitor promotion Advertising aimed at getting particular visitors to visit the exhibition.

Visual A full colour presentation drawing produced to show the client the designer's intentions for his exhibition stand.

Wall panels *See* Stock panels.

'Water and waste' Slang term covering provision of plumbing to exhibit (UK).

Weight Spread and point.

Wet mounting Process of wetting photo blow-up prior to pasting and wrapping it around panel.

Window dresser The person who actually places and displays the exhibits within the exhibition stand (UK).

Working drawings Plans, elevations, sections and detailed drawings which communicate the designer's intentions to the contractor.

Working rule agreements The official agreements between the exhibition industry, its workforce and their trade unions, published by the National Joint Council for the Exhibition Industry (UK).

Wrap mounting The process of actually carrying a face-mounted finish, usually photographic or fabric, around the edges and trapping it on the rear face of a panel. This is a method particularly used to stop photographs and other finishes peeling off the corners of a panel, as it effectively traps the material between the panel and the supporting wall.

X-height The height of a lower case character (normally measured on the height of the lower case 'x'), without ascenders or descenders, used to specify the height of lettering. *See also* Caps.

Index